NEW YORK STATE GRADE 5 SOCIAL STUDIES TEST

Second Edition

SHARON ANDREWS SZEGLOWSKI, M. ED.

BARRON'S

Dedication

- To my grandparents, for teaching me about World War II, which they lived through, and for helping me to learn the lessons that history teaches us.
- To my parents, for taking the time to talk with me and for helping me to understand and learn about the world around me.
- To my husband, who has always believed in me and with whom I celebrate each day.
- To my sons, Ian and Owen, who are the future of our world. Their love, spirit, enthusiasm, and curiosity fill me with wonder every day. I know that our future is in caring hands.

All inquiries should be addressed to:
Barron's Educational Series, Inc.
250 Wireless Boulevard
Hauppauge, New York 11788
www.barronseduc.com

ISBN-13: 978-0-7641-4025-9
ISBN-10: 0-7641-4025-6

Library of Congress Catalog Card No. 2008017014

Library of Congress Cataloging-in-Publication Data

Szeglowski, Sharon Andrews.
   New York State Grade 5 Social Studies Test / Sharon Andrews Szeglowski.—2nd ed.
          p.   cm.
   Includes index.
   ISBN-13: 978-0-7641-4025-9
   ISBN-10: 0-7641-4025-6
 1. Social sciences—Study and teaching (Elementary)—New York (State)
2. New York State Social Studies Test—Study guides.   3. Social sciences—New York (State)—Examinations, questions, etc.   4. Fifth grade (Education)—New York (State)   I. Title.   II. Title: Grade 5 Social Studies Test.

   LB1584 .S94 2008
   372.83′044—dc22   2008017014

Printed in the United States of America
9 8 7 6 5 4 3 2 1

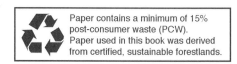

Contents

How This Book Will Help You to Prepare for the New York State Social Studies Test

Congratulations! You have taken an important step to help prepare yourself for the New York State Grade 5 Social Studies Test. You are reading this book!

This book will help you in many ways.

- You will understand why you are taking the test and how it will be graded.
- You will understand the different types of questions that you will be asked and learn strategies and hints about how to answer them.
- You will have many opportunities to answer practice questions and take whole practice exams. Then you will find detailed explanations of the correct answers.
- The appendices of this book will provide you with some important information. You will find overviews of the Grade 3 and 4 curriculums to help guide your review. Also included is a great vocabulary section with the definitions of important social studies terms.
- Throughout the book you will find hints and strategies to help you with this test.

Whether you are working through this book in school, at home with a grown-up, or on your own, I hope that this guide will help you to feel confident and prepared as you take the Social Studies Test. Good luck and happy reading!

Chapter 2

What Is the New York State Grade 5 Social Studies Test and Why Am I Taking It?

If you were a student in New York State last year, I am sure that you remember taking the New York State English Language Arts (ELA) Test, the New York State Math Test, and the New York State Science Test. Maybe you wondered then why the only subject that you didn't have to take a test in was Social Studies. Maybe you thought they forgot. Sorry, no such luck! The New York State Social Studies Test that you will be taking is really a part of this group of tests. But, I think you will agree that there were already enough tests in Grade 4, so this one is given in the fall of your fifth-grade year.

But why do you have to take all these tests in the first place? These tests are really a great thing for you. I know this may be hard to believe, so let me explain. All New York State high school students have to take some tests called the New York State Regents Exams. You have to pass these tests in order to graduate from high school. As you can tell, that makes them pretty important. They measure the skills that New York State thinks are important for you to have as you leave school and head toward your future.

Well, if these tests are so important, it seems that we ought to make sure that we do everything that we can to help you to be successful at them. One way that we can do this is by checking in with New York State students throughout their school careers and making sure that they are on the right track. In Grades 3 through 8 you will take these New York State Tests. The Social Studies tests are given in Grades 5 and 8.

These tests ask you questions about things that you have learned about in school since kindergarten. It is a way to check your progress and to see if you know and remember as much as the average fourth or fifth grader should.

If you do, then great! You will keep learning, and New York State will check in with you in eighth grade to see that you are still doing all right.

But what happens if you don't do very well? Don't panic! That is the point of the test. If your score isn't as high as it needs to be, then your school will find a way to get you help on the things that you are having trouble with. That way, by the time that you get to eighth grade, you will have had about three years of extra help where you need it.

This is a great system! Both you and your school will know where you are doing well and where you might need a little extra help. Imagine what might happen if we didn't do this, and when you got to the final Regents Exams in high school, you discovered that you needed to work on some things. Think of all the wasted years where you could have been getting extra help!

As you can see, this is a very useful test. And, if it makes you feel better, every fifth grader in New York State has to take it too!

Chapter 3

What Will the Test Be Like?

WHAT ARE THE PARTS OF THE TEST?

The New York State Social Studies Test is divided into three parts, with three different types of questions. These parts are:

- Thirty-five multiple-choice questions,
- Three or four constructed response questions,
- One document-based essay question.

We will learn a lot more about each of these types of questions, including hints and strategies, later on in this book. You will also have a chance to practice a lot of questions of each type.

You will take the Social Studies Test on two days. On each day you will have 90 minutes to complete that section of the test. On the first day, you will complete the multiple-choice and constructed response questions. On the second day, you will complete the document-based essay question.

WHAT DO I NEED TO KNOW FOR THE TEST?

This is a tricky question to answer, so before we do, I want to talk a little bit about social studies. We learn about social studies so that we will understand the way that the world works when we grow up. We will understand how our government works and what our responsibilities as citizens are. We will understand about money and trade. We will be familiar with geography and how to get from one place to another. We will understand why things are the way they are by learning about things from the past.

When you think about social studies this way, you can see that you have been learning social studies since kindergarten and even before you came to school! For example, when you learned to share your toy cars with your brother, you were learning about fairness and justice! When you found out that an exciting new toy was sold out before you got to buy one, you were learning about the principle of scarcity.

So, as surprising as it may seem, the way to answer the question of what you need to know for the test is that it will cover everything that you have learned about throughout your whole life. But that answer seems a little too big; let's see if we can narrow it down a little bit.

CONCEPTS, SKILLS, AND CONTENT COVERED ON THE TEST

As I just explained, social studies is really in everything that we do, from shopping to playing. But most people like to organize social studies into three groups or categories:

- Concepts (the big ideas)
- Skills
- Content (the facts)

The first category, *concepts*, includes the major ideas that are important to understand about the world. These concepts are the big ideas that help us to understand the new facts that we learn. They are the organizers. As we learn new information, we add it to what we already know about a concept, and it helps us to understand it even more clearly. Nationalism is one of these concepts. Nationalism is the feeling of pride that you have in your country. Every time that you learn about something that has happened in history, it might add to your pride in our country. When you learn about how our government works and the rights that you have as a citizen, it helps to build your sense of nationalism. This isn't something that you can learn about in one week; it is a lifelong idea that you are continuing to add to. To see a list of all of the concepts in the New York State Social Studies core curriculum you can look at Appendix D in the back of this book.

Another part of social studies is the *skills* that you need to develop in order to understand the world and new events as they happen. These include things like organizing events in chronological order, using reference materials to research, communicating your ideas using well-organized essays that include details to support your thoughts, and analyzing data from charts and graphs. These skills aren't facts that you need to memorize; skills help you to understand and learn new information. For example, when you search through an atlas to see where your grandparents just sent you a postcard from, you are using a reference book. You have been practicing your skills for years and will continue to get better at it as you grow up.

The last part of social studies is the facts or *content*! There is certain information that all people should know. You should be able to answer questions like, who were the first settlers in New York? What is the Constitution? What are Rain Forests like? You have learned these facts in school. The good news is that the fact questions will only be about things that you have learned in Grades 3 and 4. Even though this test takes place in Grade 5, you will not be tested on material from your Grade 5 social studies class. To remind yourself of what you learned in grades 3 and 4, you can check in Appendix B and Appendix C of this book. They list all the content that you covered in these grades. You can use it as an outline of the facts that you will need to review for the test.

You can see that social studies is a combination of three things: concepts (the big ideas), skills, and content (the facts). The New York State Social Studies Test will cover all three of these areas. So, returning to our original question, what do you need to know for the test? You need to know a combination of concepts, skills, and content. Some questions will measure what you can do, your skills. For example, you might have to read a graph and answer a question. Some questions will be checking your understanding of those big ideas. They may ask you to give an example of how we show our national pride. And finally, some questions might be checking to see if you have learned the facts.

HOW WILL THE TEST BE SCORED?

If you were in New York State for Grades 3 and 4, you will remember taking the tests for English language arts, mathematics, and science. Those tests were scored in a similar way to the social studies exam. To understand the scoring, it is important to remember the purpose of these tests, as discussed in Chapter 2.

New York State wants to know if you are understanding the concepts, skills, and content of the social studies curriculum, or if you could use a little extra help in one of those areas. Therefore, your grade will be given as a level of performance: 1, 2, 3, or 4. A score of a 1 or a 2 will indicate that you could use some support in social studies. The following chart will remind you of what these levels of performance mean.

Level of Performance	What Does It Mean?
1 Not meeting the standards	Your performance on the test does not show that you understand the concepts, skills, or content of the social studies program.
2 Not completely meeting the standards	Your performance on the test shows that you may understand some but not all of the concepts, skills, and content of the social studies program.
3 Meeting the standards	Your performance shows that you understand the concepts, skills, and content of the social studies program.
4 Meeting the standards with distinction	Your performance shows that you have an outstanding understanding of all of the concepts, skills, and content of the social studies program.

To calculate your level of performance, you will receive scores for each section of the test. You will be given credit for each of the multiple-choice questions that you answer correctly. The constructed response questions will be scored according to a scale. That means that the different parts of these questions will be worth different amounts. The scaffolding questions within the document-based essay will also earn you points. The document-based essay is scored according to a rubric. You will be graded on the content and the organization of your essay. In other words, you will be graded on what you say and how you say it.

These scores are combined to give you a raw score of between 1 and 100. The breakdown for performance levels will be similar to the one outlined here.

Performance Level	Raw Score
1	0-57
2	58-64
3	65-84
4	85-100

A Note to Teachers: For more detailed information about the scoring of the New York State Social Studies Test, please visit the NYS Department of Education's Web site at *www.emsc.nysed.gov/osa/elintsocst.html*. It is important to stay updated regarding changes to the scoring process. For example, the rubric used for scoring DBQ essays was revised for the November 2007 exam. This new rubric is available at the Web site.

SOME FINAL THOUGHTS ABOUT GRADING

As you think about grades and what they mean, you should realize that this test is just one measure of how you are doing in school. Yes, it is important, but I am sure that your parents, teachers, and friends would agree that other things are also important. Do you love to play the violin? Do you like playing soccer? Do you enjoy making your friends laugh? All of these things are important, too.

So as you read this book, try not to get too nervous. If you are concentrating on reading this book, then one thing is for sure—you are getting as prepared as you can possibly be for this test. That should make you feel great!

If you are trying your best, then whatever score you receive will truly show your strengths and weaknesses in social studies. The best thing to remember about weaknesses is that many people are willing to help you to improve. So relax and try your hardest, which is all anyone can ask of you!

Chapter 4

Strategies and Hints for Answering Multiple-Choice Questions

WHAT IS A MULTIPLE-CHOICE QUESTION?

I know that you have answered multiple-choice questions before! These are the ones where you are asked a question and then given several answers to choose from. You will remember that there were multiple-choice questions on the New York State tests you have taken before. In this chapter, we'll review the strategies and hints that will help you to answer multiple-choice questions successfully. You may already know some of them, and I hope you'll learn some new ones, too. Let's refresh your memory as we look at a sample multiple-choice question.

Sample 1

Which of the following countries set up the first colony in what is now New York State?

A. Spain
B. The Netherlands
C. England
D. The United States

The correct answer is Choice B, The Netherlands. That country set up a colony for fur trading and named the colony "New Netherland."

WHAT KINDS OF MULTIPLE-CHOICE QUESTIONS WILL THEY ASK?

When you begin to think about multiple-choice questions and look at lots of examples, you will realize that they tend to ask certain kinds of questions. Multiple-choice–style questions are mainly used:

- To see if you remember important ideas about social studies content from Grades 3 and 4
- To see if you understand social studies vocabulary words
- To see if you have mastered social studies skills, such as reading maps, graphs, charts, and so on

HOW CAN I PREPARE FOR THE MULTIPLE-CHOICE SECTION OF THE TEST?

You may think that this is a difficult part of the test to prepare for. Actually just the opposite is true. This is probably the easiest part of the test to prepare for. You just need to understand the different kinds of questions that will be on the test and know how to best prepare for each of them.

The first type of question is designed to see if you can remember the key details about the social studies topics that you have studied. It is important to realize that the test makers are interested in whether you remember the really important ideas about an event, not minor details. For example, you may be asked whom the Colonists were fighting against at the Battle of Lexington, not what day the fighting started. Once you understand this, you will realize that focusing on the main ideas is the best way to review for the test. Another important thing to remember is that they will only ask about things that all fifth graders in New York State have learned about. This will make preparing for the test easier.

So how do you know what the big, important events are? Included in this book in Appendix B and Appendix C, you will find the social studies curriculum outlines for Grades 3 and 4. These are made to tell the teachers what *all* third and fourth graders should learn about, so it makes sense that these are the topics that will be on the test. You can review these outlines to remember what you have learned in school. Also, don't forget to dust off those old study guides, projects, and books to help you refresh your memory. If you see something that you can't remember anything about, ask a teacher or visit your local library and find a book to read on the subject.

The second type of question is to check if you understand social studies vocabulary. In Appendix A, you will find a list of common vocabulary words and their definitions. It is a good idea to review these words in the weeks before the test. You might want to make flashcards as a study tool. Put the vocabulary word on one side and the definition on the other. If you can, draw a picture to illustrate the definition. This is especially helpful for geography words. You can use these cards to play a game. Turn the cards so that the word is showing. Try to define the word, and then turn it over to check yourself. If you are right, give yourself a point. Challenge yourself to increase the number of points that you earn in each review session. If you are studying with a friend, challenge each other to see who can get the most points.

The third type of multiple-choice question asks you to demonstrate a skill such as reading graphs and charts or using a compass rose. The best way to prepare for these questions is to practice! You are already doing that by reading this book . . . great job! As you go through the sample questions in this chapter and the sample tests in Chapters 7 and 8, keep track of the ones that need a skill that you have trouble with. If you don't remember how to do something, ask a teacher or a parent to help you.

Remember, they can help you now, but they won't be able to help if you don't ask until the test!

WHAT STRATEGIES CAN I USE TO ANSWER THE MULTIPLE-CHOICE QUESTIONS?

The most important strategy that you should use when you are answering multiple-choice questions is to *read very, very carefully*. Students often miss questions because they don't read the question carefully, not because they don't know the material. You should read and re-read the question to be sure that you know what they are asking you. Let's look at an example.

Sample 2

Which of the following is not a symbol of patriotism in our country?

A. the flag
B. the Pledge of Allegiance
C. the Atlantic Ocean
D. the American eagle

What do you think would happen if someone didn't read this question carefully? That's right, they wouldn't see the word "not," and they would look for the choice that does show a symbol of patriotism in our country.

That leads me right into the next hint. *Read all of the choices*! Oftentimes, students read only until they see what they think is the right answer. Going back to our example, a student who is not being careful would read only Choice A, the flag, and say, "Yes, that is a symbol of our country." Of course, this is the wrong answer. Take another look at Sample Question 2. Read it carefully. Notice that it asks you which item is *not* a symbol of patriotism in our country. This means that there will be three symbols of patriotism. Now, read all the choices. Choices A, B, and D are symbols of patriotism. If you are reading and you realize that there seem to be several correct answers, you should re-read that question. Because all the other choices are symbols of patriotism, Choice C, the Atlantic Ocean, must be the correct answer. As you can see, it is very important to read the question and all the choices very carefully.

Another strategy that works very well for multiple-choice questions is to *eliminate or cross out the answers that don't make sense.* Let's try this strategy with another example.

Sample 3

Which of the following lists includes all basic human needs?

A. food, blankets, families, TV, shelter
B. water, food, shelter, oxygen
C. shelter, friends, school, food
D. water, food, video games, books, malls

This question is a classic example of how eliminating choices can help you to decide which is the best answer. I hope that you have already read the question and all the choices very carefully. If not, go back and re-read them! We'll answer this question together by crossing-out or eliminating the choices that don't make sense or that you know are wrong.

This question asks which answer is a list of basic human needs. Hopefully, you will have noticed that there are some silly answers. Choice A, for example, contains the word "TV." We all know that although many people have TVs, they do not need them for survival. Remember that the definition of a basic human need is something you need to survive, in other words, you would die without it. So we can eliminate Choice A.

Are there any other answers that are silly? Hopefully, you said D. Choice D includes both video games and malls. Again, we would not die without these things, so we can eliminate D. That means that the correct answer is either Choice B or Choice C. Just by eliminating silly choices, we have reduced this question to only two possible choices.

Now here is where it gets tricky. The people who write these questions like to have at least two answers that are reasonable. What does that mean? Reasonable answers aren't silly or clearly wrong as Choices A and D are. Test makers do this because they want to know if you really know and understand the material or if you are just guessing. But it isn't so bad because only one answer will be completely correct. Think back for a minute; the question asks which is a list of basic needs. We know that basic needs are the things that we would die without. So let's read the choices again.

B. water, food, shelter, oxygen
C. shelter, friends, school, food

You would die without all of the items in Choice B. What about the items in Choice C? Even though all of these things are important, we wouldn't die without them . . . even school! Eliminating the answers that you know are wrong can help you to narrow down your search for the right answer.

A FEW OTHER THOUGHTS ABOUT MULTIPLE-CHOICE QUESTIONS

Kids often wonder what they should do if they narrow down their choices and still can't decide on the right answer. A great suggestion is to leave that question, go on to the next question, and come back to it later. When you take a break and clear your mind, you may be able to see the correct answer later. Be sure that you skip the question on your answer sheet if you do this; otherwise, you might start putting the answers in the wrong spot and get them all wrong! A good way to avoid this error is to check yourself every so often to make sure that the question you just read matches the number on the answer sheet. If you get into trouble with numbering, let your teacher know.

If you still don't know the answer when you come back to the question, then narrow it down to as few choices as possible and guess. This is certainly not the ideal strategy, but sometimes, when you have a "gut feeling" about something, it turns out to be right. Besides, if you leave it blank it will be marked wrong anyway, so take a shot at it!

One final thing to consider is time. You will have 90 minutes to complete about 35 multiple-choice and three or four constructed response questions. You will learn all about constructed response questions in the next chapter. You will probably need about 30 minutes to complete the constructed response questions, so you should have about 60 minutes for the multiple-choice questions. If you do the math, that comes out to a little under 2 minutes per question. You don't need to time yourself or get too worried, but you do need to realize what that means. It means that if you spend 5 to 10 minutes on one question, you could easily run out of time later. The questions that you don't finish will all be marked wrong. So don't get stuck on one question! It is a good idea to check yourself after about half an hour to see if you are finished with about half of the multiple-choice questions. If you are working on Question 17 or 18, you are on schedule. If you haven't gotten that far, you will need to pick up the pace. If you are ahead of that, make sure that you are taking enough time to read carefully. Of course, these are just suggestions to give you an idea of how to pace yourself on a timed test.

Try these multiple-choice questions using the strategies that we just reviewed. Then we will check the answers.

Sample 4

One of the Native American Groups found in New York State is called the

A. Sioux.
B. Clans.
C. Adirondacks.
D. Iroquois (Hodenosaunee).

Sample 5

Which of the following is a fact that proves that our country's government is a democracy?

A. All people over the age of 18 can vote.
B. In New York State, you can drive at the age of 16.
C. We have never had a woman president.
D. Washington, D.C. is our country's capital.

Sample 6

Population of Selected States on April 1, 2000

State Name	Population in 2000
New York	18,976,457
Maine	1,274,923
Kansas	2,688,418
Alaska	626,932
Texas	20,851,820

Data Source: U.S. Census Bureau

Which of the states listed below had the highest population in the year 2000?

A. New York
B. Kansas
C. Alaska
D. Maine

Let's look at the correct answers to these questions. The correct answer for Sample 4 was Choice D. How did you do? You can eliminate Choice B because Clan is not a tribe name; it is the name of the family structure in Iroquois tribes. You can also eliminate Choice C because the Adirondacks is also not a tribe name; it is the name of the mountain range in the Northeastern part of New York State. That leaves Choices A and D as our reasonable choices. While the Sioux are a Native American tribe, they are found in the great plains of our country. Hopefully, you remember learning about the Iroquois. Choice D is the correct answer.

The correct answer to Sample 5 is Choice A. When you read this question carefully, you see that it is asking for a fact to prove or show how our country is a democracy. Remember, a democracy is a government that is run for the people, by the people. While Choices B, C, and D are all facts, they don't give an example of people being part of our government. The only choice that does that is A, so it is the correct answer. The fact that we vote shows that we are a part of our government. It is a way that we have a chance to express our opinion.

The correct answer to Sample 6 is Choice A. This question asks you to use the skill of reading a chart for information. The tricky part of this question is that, if you don't read it carefully, you might think that the answer is Texas. Texas does have the highest population on the chart. However, the question asks which of the states listed below had the highest population, not which of the states in the charts. Remember to read carefully!

To practice more multiple-choice questions, go to Appendix G.

Chapter 5

Strategies and Hints for Answering Constructed Response Questions

WHAT IS A CONSTRUCTED RESPONSE QUESTION?

When you take the New York State Social Studies Test, Part One, you will be asked to complete three or four constructed response questions. Some people call these CRQs for short. Although you might not have heard the name before, you have probably seen lots of questions like these on science tests, math tests, and other social studies tests.

Let's think about the name: constructed response questions. What does it mean? Basically, you will "construct" or build your answers in response to a series of questions. To do this, you will be given some help. This help will be some type of document. A document is anything that provides you with data or ideas about a certain topic. It could be a picture, graph, chart, map, poster, journal entry, or timeline. It might even be a poem, cartoon, or song. Although documents can be many different things, they have one thing in common. They give you lots of information that helps you to build the answer to the question. **The documents are the clues!**

A constructed response question isn't really one question at all. It is a document followed by a series of questions, usually three. Later in this chapter, we will explore some tips and strategies that you can use to answer these questions successfully.

But before we go much farther, let's look at a sample constructed response question.

Sample 1

Directions: Please use your knowledge of social studies and this document to answer Questions 1–3.

Continent Name	Population Estimate for 2000
North America	476,000,000
South America	343,000,000
Europe	727,000,000
Asia	3,641,000,000
Africa	778,000,000
Australia and Oceania	30,000,000
Antarctica	0

1. What was the population of South America in 2000?

   _____

   _____

2. How many more people lived in North America than in Australia and Oceania in 2000?

   _____

   _____

3. Why does Antarctica have the lowest population of all the continents?

   _____

   _____

WHAT TYPES OF CONSTRUCTED RESPONSE QUESTIONS WILL THEY ASK?

As you begin to get familiar with constructed response questions, you might notice that the questions are set up to follow a pattern. Understanding this pattern will help you to answer the questions and to give excellent answers. The pattern usually looks like this.

The first question is usually the easiest of the three questions. It asks you to look at the document and find the answer. The answer is almost always right in the document so that you don't have to search too hard or remember the answer from class. This question is like a hide-and-seek game. Read the question, be sure that you know what to look for, and then you're off, searching to find the answer! Let's look at Sample 1. The first question was:

What was the population of South America in 2000?

When you answer this question you will need to look carefully at the chart.

Continent Name	Population Estimate for 2000
North America	476,000,000
South America	**343,000,000**
Europe	727,000,000

You can see that the left column gives the continent's name and the right column gives the estimated population for the year 2000. To answer this question, you first need to find South America in the left column and then read across to the right to see that the population was 343,000,000. Did you get it right? Great job!

The second question in the pattern usually asks you to look at the document and find some information in the document much as you did in the first question, but then you have to do something with that information. You might have to compare two pieces of data to see which one is greater, or you might have to make a generalization based on that data. The second question often involves a little more work than the first question, but the information is right on the page for you. This is a chance for you to use your math, reading, and thinking skills. In Sample 1, the second question was:

How many more people lived in North America than in Australia and Oceania in 2000?

The words "how many more" are usually a clue that you will need to do some math. In this example you will need to find the population of North America, which is 476,000,000, and the population of Australia and Oceania, which is 30,000,000. To see how many more people lived in North America, you will need to subtract Australia and Oceania's population from North America's. Set up your problem like this:

476,000,000	Number of people in North America
− 30,000,000	Minus number of people in Australia and Oceania
446,000,000	Equals your answer!

446,000,000 more people lived in North America than in Australia and Oceania. All the information that you needed to find the answer was hidden right in the document. To get the answer, you just had to find it and use your math skills.

The third question in the pattern is what I like to call the "thinker question." These questions usually ask you to use the information from the document and what you have learned in school to answer a question. The idea is that the first two questions have been helping you to remember what you have learned about a topic in school and now you get a chance to use that knowledge to answer a third question. Looking at Sample 1, you can see that the third question was:

Why does Antarctica have the lowest population of all the continents?

When you see this question you will notice that it starts with "Why." This is usually a sure sign that you are going to have to do some thinking! The answer to this question is not in the document; it is inside your head. You might remember learning about the continents and their locations in third grade. Did you remember that Antarctica is the continent that includes the South Pole? Picture that place in your head. Why wouldn't anybody live there? Of course, the answer is that the environment is one that is very hard for human beings to live in. It is just too cold!

Let's review the CRQ pattern again:

Question 1	The answer is usually right in the document.
Question 2	The information that you need is usually in the document, but you may have to do something with that data.
Question 3	The thinker question usually asks you to remember something about the topic from what you have learned in school.

It is important to note that *not* all CRQs will follow this exact pattern. However, these are the three types of questions that you will most likely be asked. For example, they might give you two questions that follow the pattern for Question 2 and no thinker question. But, once you get used to these three types of questions, you will be ready for anything!

HOW DO I ANALYZE THE DOCUMENT THAT THEY GIVE ME?

Analyzing a document sounds very clever and quite hard, but it really isn't! It is just very fancy language that tells you to look at the document carefully and try to figure out what it means. This is something that you have been doing your whole life! When you see a poster for a new movie, you read it and figure out what the movie is about, who is in it, and when it starts. You just analyzed a document! When you go to a restaurant and read a menu, you see what the names of the foods are, what is in them, and how much they cost. Once again, you have just analyzed a document. The only difference is that this time the documents are about something that you have learned in social studies class. Remember, these documents are there to help you to "construct" or build your answer . . . so pay attention to them. They are your clues! Although you analyze documents every day, there are some tips that you will want to remember for different kinds of documents. Let's take a look at how to approach some of these documents.

Charts

1. Read the title carefully. The title tells you what the chart is about. It is very important!
2. Carefully read the columns of the chart to see what information is in each part. Charts can be organized differently, so it is important to make sure that you understand how the chart that you are given is set up.

3. Pay close attention to any information that strikes you as interesting or unusual. You may be asked a question about it!

4. Think about what you have learned in class about the topic of this chart. You may need this information to help you answer some of the questions.

Maps

1. Read the title of the map. It can give you lots of information about the map's location and what time period is being shown.

2. Look at the map key or legend to see what the symbols mean. Even though you may see some familiar symbols, they may have different meanings on this map.

3. Look at the scale of miles and the compass rose; they can give you important information about the map, and you may have to use them later.

4. Look at the map and look for any familiar places on the map. Think about what you have learned about these locations.

Graphs

1. Read the title. The title of a graph should clearly explain what data it contains.

2. Think about what type of graph it is and what that type of graph is used for. This can give you lots of clues. For example, line graphs are usually used to show a change in something over time, while a pie graph or circle graph is used to show percentages of a whole.

3. Look carefully at the graph and read all the labels on it. Really spend some time understanding how this graph is organized.

4. Think about everything that you have learned about the subject shown in the graph.

Timelines

1. If the timeline has a title, read it carefully. It should tell you exactly what the timeline is about.
2. Look at the beginning and ending years of the graph to get an idea of how many years are covered by the timeline.
3. Look at the events that are marked on the timeline.
4. Think about anything that you know about the time period being shown on the timeline.

Photographs/Paintings

1. Look to see if the photograph has a title or a caption. If it does, read it carefully and look for any clues that it gives you about the subject of the photograph.
2. Look at the photograph carefully. Who is in it? Are they famous? What are they doing? When do you think the photograph was taken? Why did somebody want to capture this person or event in a painting or photograph?
3. Think about anything that you know about the person or people in the picture or the event that is taking place.

Quotations

1. Read any information given about the quotation. For example, who said it? When and where was it said? This information is sometimes written directly after the quotation and can help you to understand the quotation when you read it better.
2. Read the quotation and think about it. What did the person say? Why might they have said this? Who were they saying it to? When did the person say this?
3. Think about anything that you know about the person who said the quotation or the event or subject that they were talking about.

Pieces of Text

1. Figure out what type of text you are about to read. Is it a journal entry? A poem? A part of a book? Words to a song?

2. Read the text. Who is the author? What is the author saying? Why might he say that? What event or subject is he talking about?

3. Think about anything that you know about the author or the topic that he is writing about.

SAMPLE QUESTIONS: LET'S TRY SOME TOGETHER

Now that you understand what types of questions you might see and have some tips to analyze the documents to help you to answer them, let's try a sample question. In Sample 2, we will follow all the suggested steps together.

Sample 2

Directions: *Please use your knowledge of social studies and the quotation to answer Questions 1–3.*

We must unite ourselves into one common band of brothers. We must have but one voice. Many voices makes confusion. We must have one fire, one pipe, and one war club. This will give us strength.

~The words of Hiawatha, an Onondaga Chief, as he spoke to representatives of the Seneca, Cayuga, Onondaga, Oneida, and Mohawk tribes sometime in the 1550s.

1. What tribe of Native Americans is Hiawatha from?

_____

_____

_____

_____

_____

2. Give one reason why Hiawatha says that the tribes should unite.

_____

_____

_____

_____

_____

3. When these tribes did unite, what was the name of the group that they formed?

_____

_____

_____

_____

_____

Let's work through this CRQ together. When you first look at this document, you can see that it is text, but what kind of text? We need to first figure out whether this is a song, poem, quotation, story, or something else. In this example, we can tell that it is a quotation because underneath the text box it says these are "the words of." Reading about who said this will help you to think about what they meant and why they said it. This quotation is from Hiawatha. The document tells us that he was an Onondaga chief, speaking to representatives of the Seneca, Cayuga, Onondaga, Oneida, and Mohawk tribes. We are also told that this quotation is from the 1550s.

Now read the quotation. Take the time to re-read the quotation slowly so that you are sure that you understand it. This quotation talks about the importance of joining together to be stronger.

The next thing you should do is to think about the quotation. It should remind you of the things that you have learned about in school. In fourth grade you learned about the Native American Tribes in New York joining together to form the Iroquois Confederacy. This made them very strong. The original tribes were the Cayuga, Onondaga, Mohawk, Seneca, and Oneida. Now let's try the questions.

1. *What tribe of Native Americans is Hiawatha from?*

Answer: Onondaga

Explanation: Underneath the quotation, it says that Hiawatha was an Onondaga chief. This question fits the pattern we discussed earlier. The answer is found in the document.

2. *Give one reason why Hiawatha says that the tribes should unite.*

Answer: The answer is one of the following:

• By uniting they will be stronger.
• Many voices makes confusion.

Explanation: There are two acceptable answers to this question. To find them, you must read the quotation and understand the question. The best answer is that Hiawatha is trying to convince the tribes to unite because they will be stronger together than as separate tribes. He also mentions that if they have separate voices, it leads to confusion. This is also an acceptable answer. This question follows the pattern for a second question in a constructed response question. You needed to find the information in the document, but you must also understand what Hiawatha was saying to answer the question.

3. *When these tribes did unite, what was the name of the group that they formed?*

Answer: The Iroquois Confederacy

Explanation: This is the thinker question, where you need to bring in your own knowledge. **The document gives you clues.** It tells you the tribe names and also why they united. This information should remind you of what you learned in fourth grade about the Iroquois Confederacy. This question follows the pattern for a third question in a CRQ.

To practice more constructed response questions, go to Appendix G.

Chapter 6

Strategies and Hints for Answering Document-Based Essay Questions

WHAT IS A DOCUMENT-BASED ESSAY QUESTION?

On the second day of the New York State Social Studies Test, you will be asked to complete one question that is called a document-based essay question. Your teachers will probably call these DBQs because that is much easier to say!

The good news about DBQs is that you will only have to do one, and you will have 90 minutes to complete it. That may sound like a lot of time for just one question, but it is actually just right because a DBQ has many different parts. You'll have to put your thinking cap on to make sure that you come up with a clear and accurate essay.

In this chapter, we will discuss all the steps that you need to complete to answer a DBQ. Pay close attention and you are sure to learn some helpful hints and clever strategies too!

WHAT ARE THE PARTS OF A DBQ?

On the first page of a DBQ, you will be given the directions. Basically, the directions will tell you that you will need to analyze some documents, answer questions about those documents, and finally write an essay. Of course, you'll use your knowledge of social studies as well as this series of documents to help you answer the essay question.

After these directions, you will be given historical background information. This contains a few sentences that will give you some useful information related to the topic of your essay question. Remember to go back and re-read this section before you start your essay because there will probably be a few facts that you will want to include in your essay!

After a few more directions, the last thing that you will see on the first page is your essay topic. Sometimes this will be in a box to help it stand out. This is the most important thing on the page! All of the other parts of the DBQ are really just to help you to think about, and answer, the essay topic in the box.

Let's take a break for a minute and then look at what the first page of a real DBQ might look like.

Sample DBQ A

Directions: The following task is based on Documents 1–6. This task will check your ability to work with historical documents. Look at each document carefully and answer the question or questions that follow. Use your answers to the questions to help you write your essay.

Historical background: America has been seen by many as a land of opportunity. Over time many people from all over the world have made America their home.

Task:

For Part A, read each document carefully and answer the question or questions after it. Then read the directions for Part B and write your essay.

For Part B, using the information from the documents, your answers to Part A, and your knowledge of social studies, write a well-organized essay. In your essay, you should:

> Describe why America is often called a land of immigrants and some of the reasons that these immigrants may have chosen America as their home.

You should recognize some of the different parts of the DBQ question that we just discussed and see that the information on the first page will tell you what you are expected to write about. Following the directions, you'll see that the historical background section is giving you some information that is related to the essay topic. Remember that the most important thing on the page is the essay topic, which is easy to spot in the box.

In this example you are asked to write about immigrants coming to America and the reasons that they may have come. You will probably remember learning about this in fourth grade. It is a very interesting subject. Later on, you will be writing that essay. But before you begin writing, you should be happy to know that there is some help on the way!

The next several pages of the test will include a series of five to seven documents that will help you write your essay. In Chapter 5, we learned a lot about documents. Remember, documents are really just tools that give you ideas or data about a topic. You'll remember that we looked at charts, diagrams, quotations, photographs, and other types of documents. **Just like in the constructed response questions, these documents are your clues.** They are carefully chosen to give you information that will help you write your essay. Each one will give you valuable facts and ideas that will make your essay answer more detailed.

As you look at each document, you should analyze it carefully by following the steps that we discussed in Chapter 5. You will notice that each document will be followed by a question. These questions are called *scaffolding questions*. Have you heard the word scaffolding before? It is a platform that is used to hold up a person as he or she works on building something. These questions are designed to hold you up, too. They are written to make you analyze each document and pull out the important information.

The scaffolding questions help you in three ways. First, they help you to analyze the document and find the clues and information in the document. They also help you put your ideas into sentences that you can use when you're writing your essay. The third way that these questions help you is that they give you a way to earn some points. Your answers to these scaffolding questions will be graded as a part of your overall DBQ score; answering this part carefully is an easy way to build up your score as you build up your knowledge about the essay topic.

After you have analyzed each of the documents and completed the scaffolding questions, it is finally time to write your essay. The next page in the test will remind you of the essay topic and then you will be given a blank planning page. This planning page is a great place to write a simple outline of your essay, to jot down key ideas, and to organize your thoughts before you write.

The final pages of the DBQ will be lined pages that you will use to write your actual essay on.

We started this chapter by saying that you will only have to answer one DBQ. But as you can see, there are many parts to it. Remember that all the documents and scaffolding questions are there to help you to write a great essay. Later on in the chapter, we will look at a complete sample DBQ and answer it together.

WHAT TYPES OF QUESTIONS WILL THEY ASK?

Before we try completing a DBQ, it is important to think about what types of essay questions you might be asked. The DBQ section of the test is the place where you will be asked about those concepts or "big ideas" that you have learned about throughout your social studies education. You will not be asked about small details. Think about it; how could you write an entire essay about a few facts?

For example, what would you be able to write about a question like, "What was the name of the last battle of the Revolutionary War?" Your essay would only need to be a few words long to answer that it was the Battle of Yorktown. By now you probably realize that this type of question would most likely be found in the multiple-choice section of the test.

Instead, DBQ questions will tend to be the "Why" questions or the "How" questions. You could be asked to show how something has changed over time or to discuss different people's opinions about the same event. You might be asked to compare and contrast two things. Or, you might have to explain the reasons why something happened. These are definitely "thinkers." To review the concepts that are developed in the New York State Social Studies program, take a look at Appendix D.

Earlier in the chapter we looked at the directions for a sample DBQ. Now we'll continue by looking at the complete question including the documents and scaffolding questions. As you go through it, try to answer each of these questions and to understand how they will help you answer the essay question at the end. Remember that all these answers will count toward your final grade. Then try writing an answer to the essay question. When you have looked at the whole DBQ, we will work through it step by step and discuss some great strategies to help you.

Sample DBQ A (continued)

Directions: The following task is based on Documents 1–6. This task will check your ability to work with historical documents. Look at each document carefully and answer the question or questions that follow. Use your answers to the questions to help you write your essay.

Historical background: America has been seen by many as a land of opportunity. Over time many people from all over the world have made America their home.

Task:

For Part A, read each document carefully and answer the question or questions after it. Then read the directions for Part B and write your essay.

For Part B, using the information from the documents, your answers to Part A, and your knowledge of social studies, write a well-organized essay. In your essay, you should:

> Describe why America is often called a land of immigrants and some of the reasons that these immigrants may have chosen America as their home.

PART A: SHORT-ANSWER QUESTIONS

Directions: *Read each document carefully and answer the question or questions that follow. Please answer the questions in the space provided.*

Document 1

The New Colossus
By Emma Lazarus

Here at our sea-washed, sunset gates shall stand
A mighty woman with a torch, whose flame
Is the imprisoned lightning, and her name
Mother of Exiles.
"Give me your tired, your poor,
Your huddled masses yearning to breathe free,
The wretched refuse of your teeming shore.
Send these, the homeless, tempest-tost to me,
I lift my lamp beside the golden door!"

~A part of this poem is engraved on the base of the Statue of Liberty.

1. List two ways used by this poem to describe the kind of people that will be welcomed by the Statue of Liberty.

   (a) _____

   (b) _____

Document 2

An Italian family waits on their ship, before being allowed to take a ferry to Ellis Island.

1. What country are the people in this picture from?

   _____

2. Where did these immigrants arrive in the United States?

   _____

   _____

Document 3

> After I first visited the United States, I wanted to live here. I came from the United Kingdom, a very free and democratic society. So, what is so special about the United States? It is very simple: the total commitment to freedom. I simply was not convinced that Europe was totally committed to defending their freedom. In a word, the USA stands for commitment. It says what it stands for and stands for what it says. No other nation in the world has this commitment to freedom.

~Gerald Andrews, Immigrant 1980

1. What does Mr. Andrews feel is so special about the United States of America?

_____

_____

_____

_____

Document 4

United States Immigration by Where They Last Lived

Region of Last Residence	1821-1830	1921-1930	1991-2000
Europe	98,797	2,463,194	1,359,737
Asia	30	112,059	2,795,672
The Americas	11,564	1,516,716	4,486,806
Africa	16	6,286	354,939
Oceania	2	8,726	55,845
Unknown	33,030	228	42,418
Total	143,439	4,107,209	9,095,417

Data Source: U.S. Department of Immigration and Naturalization

1. Did the number of immigrants increase or decrease from 1821 to 2000?

_____

2. List four regions of the world that America has welcomed people from.

_____

_____

_____

_____

Document 5

The Pledge of Allegiance

I pledge allegiance to the Flag
Of the United States of America
And to the Republic
For which it stands,
One Nation under God,
Indivisible, with liberty and justice
For all.

---

1. What is one thing that the pledge of allegiance says that the United States gives to all?

_____

_____

Document 6

The Constitution of the United States of America
Amendments I–X: The Bill of Rights

Amendment I: Freedom of religion, speech, press, and the right to petition.

Amendment II: The right to bear arms.

Amendment III: No soldier shall have to be housed and fed in people's homes, without the homeowner's consent.

Amendment IV: People and homes are protected from unreasonable searches and seizures.

Amendment V: All people are guaranteed that the charges against them be stated to a Grand Jury. A person cannot be tried twice for the same crime.

Amendment VI: All people are guaranteed a speedy and public trial.

Amendment VII: Guarantees a jury trial.

Amendment VIII: All people are guaranteed that they shall not suffer cruel and unusual punishments.

Amendment IX: Just because some rights are explained in the Constitution, it does not take away other rights that are not listed.

Amendment X: All powers that are not explained by the Constitution to be for the national government or that are not prohibited for the state shall become the powers of the states.

---

1. Based on the Bill of Rights, why might an immigrant want to become a citizen?

   _____

   _____

   _____

   _____

PART B: ESSAY

Directions: Write a well-organized essay using the documents, the answers to the questions in Part A, and your knowledge of social studies.

Historical background: America has been seen by many as a land of opportunity. Over time many people from many places have made America their home.

Task: Using information from the documents, your knowledge of social studies, and your answers to Part A, write an essay in which you:

> Describe why America is often called a land of immigrants and some of the reasons that these immigrants may have chosen America as their home.

In your essay, be sure to

- Tell places immigrants have come to the United States from.
- Tell some reasons why they might have come.
- Include details, examples, or reasons in developing your ideas.
- Use information from at least three documents in your answer (if there are an odd number of documents, use at least half).

Planning Page

Use this page to plan for your essay. Work on this page will not be counted toward your final score. Do not write your essay here.

Use the following space to write your essay.

_____

_____

_____

_____

_____

_____

_____

_____

_____

_____

_____

_____

_____

_____

_____

_____

_____

_____

_____

_____

_____

_____

DBQ STRATEGIES

I'm sure you are anxious to see how your answers compare to the sample essay, but first I want to talk about a few tools that you are allowed to use on New York State tests. I am talking about highlighting pens and self-stick removable notes. Your teacher will probably mention them to you and give you some ideas about how you can use highlighters or self-stick removable notes and help you to figure out if they will be useful for you.

First, let's talk about highlighting pens. Hopefully you have realized as you have read this book that everybody has a different test-taking style. That is great because we are all different people with different ways of doing things. Whether or not you should use a highlighter depends on how you answer this question: Will it help me or hurt me? I have seen some kids use a highlighter to highlight a few key words. Then when they are beginning to write their essay they quickly see those key words and are reminded of the important details. That might be really helpful.

But it can hurt you, too. Sometimes kids spend a long time highlighting too much, sometimes almost everything on a page! Then they have a problem! Not only is the document hard to look at, but they have wasted a lot of time too. When you go back and look at a document that has too much highlighting, you will probably not be able to find the key information that is really helpful to answer the essay question. Your own highlighting may distract you! My suggestion is to use highlighters only if you have talked about it at school and practiced using them.

What about self-stick removable notes? I actually like these a lot more than highlighting because they can really help you to organize your thoughts for the essay. After you've finished analyzing the documents and answering the scaffolding questions, re-read the essay topic. Then, go back to each document with the essay topic in mind and write down a fact or facts that you want to use in your essay, from each document, on a self-stick removable note. When you have done this with each document, you can then arrange your notes on your planning page in the order you want to write about them. This is a clever and fast way to create your outline. It is also a good way to make sure that you use information and details from all the documents. But again, everyone's style is different. This idea for using the self-stick removable notes may not work out for you. You might want to try it on one of the Sample DBQs in this book and see if you like it. It is important to find out if a tool is going to be helpful for you, or just a distraction.

Sample A: Answers and Explanations

Document 1

1. *Answer:* This question has several possible answers. The following answers are acceptable: poor, tired, huddled masses, people yearning to breathe free, the wretched refuse of your teeming shore, the homeless, and the tempest-tost.

Explanation: Be careful to choose only words that you know. For example, you probably know what poor means, and we've all been hungry before. But you may not know what tempest-tost means. Even though you would get credit for this as a correct answer, it won't help you to write the essay if you don't understand what it means.

One word of caution for this question is that you must have one answer for A and one answer for B. Do not put both answers on line A because the person scoring your paper may not think that you answered B. Remember that these answers do count toward your final essay answer.

Document 2

1. *Answer:* Italy

Explanation: The caption for the picture states that the family is Italian. Italian people are from Italy.

2. *Answer:* Ellis Island

Explanation: The caption for the picture explains that they are waiting for a ferry to take them to Ellis Island. Another acceptable answer would be New York City because that is where Ellis Island is located.

Document 3

1. *Answer:* The correct answer is: a total commitment to freedom, or similar words.

Explanation: The answer to this question can be found directly in the reading. Mr. Andrews clearly states what he believes is so special about the United States.

Document 4

1. *Answer:* Increase

Explanation: If you look at the number of immigrants in the 1821–1830 range, the total was 143,439, but in the 1991–2000 range the total was 9,095,417. This number is much greater, so the number of immigrants increased or got larger.

2. *Answer/Explanation:* To answer this question, you must list four of the following five choices: Europe, Asia, The Americas, Africa, Oceania. It is not correct if you wrote "Unknown" because even though there are people listed in that category on the graph, it is not a place or region. It just means that for some reason the government was unable to find out where these people last lived.

Document 5

1. *Answer:* There are two possible answers to this question. Either liberty or justice is acceptable. If you put both liberty and justice, that is acceptable too.

Explanation: To find the answer to this question you need to look back at the pledge and find the phrase "for all." Directly before the question, it is stated that there is liberty and justice for all.

Document 6

1. *Answer/Explanation:* There are several answers to this question. The first style of correct answer would be if you answered that an immigrant might want to become a citizen to get certain basic rights. This is a very general answer. Even though that answer is correct, there is a more specific kind of answer using information taken right from the document. This type of answer might help you more when you are writing your essay. You could also have answered that an immigrant might want to become a citizen to have freedoms such as the freedom of speech, religion, or the press.

Essay

The next page that you saw probably seemed like a repeat of the first page of the DBQ. It is! It simply gives you the essay topic again. Then you were given a planning page to use as you get ready to write your essay. If you used the self-stick removable notes, this is where you might have arranged your notes as an outline. If you did not, it is important that you took some time to make a quick plan of what you needed to include in your essay. This is a sample of what a planning page might look like.

Introduction: Use historical background and say ... America is often called a land of immigrants. This is true because ...

Body Paragraph One: Where people came from

- Where people came from: List Asia, Europe, Oceania, the Americas, and Africa.
- Two specific examples are Mr. Andrews from the United Kingdom in Europe and the Italian Family from Document 2.
- Specific details include 1821–1830 when about 30 people came from Asia and from 1991–2000 when about 2,795,672 came from Asia.

Body Paragraph Two: Why people came

- Mr. Andrews—Commitment to freedom, not leaving a bad place
- People might be leaving places they are treated badly and want the freedom
- Specific examples; freedoms of the Bill of Rights are freedom of speech, press, religion, etc.
- Might want to come to seek their fortune
- Emma Lazarus poem welcomes all people no matter if rich or poor as long as they want freedom.

Conclusion: Restate that America is a land of immigrants and that they all hope for a good future in America.

Documents I used: 1, 2, 3, 4, 5, 6

I used my planning page to create a simple outline to help me organize my thinking. You might notice that it's not important to write in complete sentences on the planning page. This saves you time. Also, this work will *not* count at all toward your final grade. It is very important not to spend so long on the planning page that you will run out of time on the essay, which is of course graded. You will not have enough time to write a whole rough draft, so an outline is a great substitute. It is important to realize that outlines work well, but only you will decide which strategy works the best for you. Use these practice DBQs to try different ways of using your planning page. In the end, just make sure that you use it!

Here's a hint that can be very useful. Look at the last part of my planning page. It says "Documents I used: 1, 2, 3, 4, 5, 6." I wrote this when I started my planning page, then each time I finished jotting down facts or notes from a specific document on my planning page, I crossed out the number from my list. I crossed it out with two lines if I used it twice, and so on. You should try to use all the documents in some way, and this is a good way to make sure you haven't skipped any of them. You will find that you use some documents more than others, but you should try to mention something from each of them. One of the directions specifically tells you to use information from at least three documents. Be sure that you do this, as it will count toward your score.

Now, take a look at what a complete essay might look like. What makes this a good essay is that it answers all of the parts of the question, it uses specific details to support the ideas, it is well organized with an introduction, body, and conclusion, and it uses information from all of the documents.

America is often called a land of immigrants, and you only need to look at our history to see why. Native Americans settled here in about 20,000 B.C. and lived undisturbed until European explorers came in the 1400s and 1500s. From that point on, our country has been a welcoming new home to immigrants from all over the world. They come from many places and for many reasons, but they have one thing in common. They all call America home.

Immigrants have been coming from many places all over the world for many years. The places that people come from have changed over the years. For example, during 1821–1830 we know that only 30 people came from Asia. But during 1991–2000 about 2,795,672 immigrants came from Asia! We have welcomed people from all parts of the world. Mr. Andrews is from the United Kingdom and the family pictured in Document 2 is from Italy. There have also been immigrants from Asia, Africa, Oceania, and the Americas. The world is welcomed into the United States.

Immigrants come to America for many reasons. Sometimes people are leaving something bad in their own country, but not always. Mr. Gerald Andrews is an example. He was impressed with America's commitment to freedom and wanted to live here ever since he visited for the first time. Sometimes, people are being treated unfairly in their home country and want to come to America for all the rights and freedoms that they will be guaranteed. For example, many people are treated badly because of their religion, but in America, the Bill of Rights and the First Amendment guarantee people the freedom to be any religion that they want. Some of the other freedoms that people will gain are freedom of speech and the press. Another reason that people come to America is to seek their fortune. You do not need to be rich to come to America. As the Emma Lazarus poem that is inscribed on the base of the Statue of Liberty says, "Give me your tired, your poor, your huddled masses yearning to breathe free." This poem is a welcome to all people.

As you can see, America has been called a land of immigrants, and it is true. We have welcomed people from all over the world. These people come for many reasons. You only need to look at the faces of the Italian family pictured in Document 2 to see hope. This family looks toward a bright future, as do all immigrants who come to the land of immigrants. They are welcomed by the Statue of Liberty and her kind words.

To practice more document-based essay questions, go to Appendix G.

Chapter 7

Let's Take a Complete Practice Test

N ow it is time to try out all the strategies and hints that you have learned. You will have 90 minutes to complete the multiple-choice and constructed response questions. You will then have another 90 minutes to do the document-based essay question.

PRACTICE TEST 1

MULTIPLE-CHOICE QUESTIONS

Directions: Please use your knowledge of social studies to choose the best answer to each of the following questions.

1. Which of the following people did not explore within the area that is now called New York State?

    A. Jacques Cartier
    B. Henry Hudson
    C. Christopher Columbus
    D. Giovanni da Verrazzano

2. Which of the following lists contains items that would all be considered natural resources?

    A. trees, lakes, coal
    B. coal, telephones, trains
    C. trains, bridges, cars
    D. horses, lightbulbs, money

3. What is the name of the battle during the Revolutionary War that is sometimes called the turning point of the war? This battle convinced the French to join the fight on the colonists' side.

    A. the Battle of Yorktown
    B. the Battle of Saratoga
    C. the Battle of Normandy
    D. the Battle of Lexington

4. Which of the following is an *opinion* about rural areas?

    A. There may be farms in rural areas.
    B. There are not many factories in rural areas.
    C. Rural areas are beautiful.
    D. Rural areas usually have a lower population than urban areas.

Base your answers to Questions 5 and 6 on the following timeline.

Major Inventions and Achievements

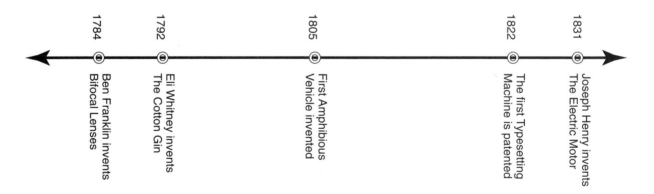

1784	1792	1805	1822	1831
Ben Franklin invents Bifocal Lenses	Eli Whitney invents The Cotton Gin	First Amphibious Vehicle invented	The first Typesetting Machine is patented	Joseph Henry invents The Electric Motor

5. Which of the inventions listed on the timeline happened first?

    A. electric motor   **C.** bifocal lenses
    B. typesetting machine   **D.** cotton gin

6. All the inventions listed on the timeline happened

   A. after the Declaration of Independence was approved.
   B. before the Declaration of Independence was approved.
   C. at the same time that the Declaration of Independence was approved.

7. Which is not an example of *goods* that a country might export?

   A. furniture
   B. cars
   C. clothing
   D. firefighters

8. A person who remained loyal to the British government during the Revolutionary War was called

   A. a loyalist.
   B. a cooper.
   C. a patriot.
   D. a blacksmith.

Please answer Questions 9 and 10 using this chart.

Selected U.S. National Parks

Park Name	State	Land Area (acres)	Interesting Feature
Yosemite	California	761,266	Contains the nation's highest waterfall
Grand Canyon	Arizona	1,217,403	Contains the spectacular canyon around the Colorado River
Denali	Alaska	4,740,912	Contains the highest mountain in the United States
Carlsbad Caverns	New Mexico	46,766	Contains largest known caverns
Mesa Verde	Colorado	52,122	Contains the best preserved prehistoric cliff dwellings in the United States

9. In what state is the national park that contains the highest mountain in the United States?

A. Colorado
B. Alaska

C. New Mexico
D. California

10. If you wanted to visit Yosemite National Park, which direction would you travel from New York State?

A. west
B. east

C. north
D. south

11. Which of the following jobs might a person in colonial New York have had?

A. farmer
B. blacksmith

C. cooper
D. All of the above.

12. On which national holiday do we honor a man who symbolizes the peaceful struggles for civil rights in America?

   A. Columbus Day
   B. Memorial Day
   C. Labor Day
   D. Martin Luther King, Jr. Day

13. New York City is

   A. a rural area.
   B. an urban area.
   C. a suburban area.
   D. the state capital of New York State.

14. The imaginary line that connects the North and South Poles runs through Greenwich, England, and marks 0 degrees longitude is known as

   A. the prime meridian.
   B. the equator.
   C. the Tropic of Capricorn.
   D. the Tropic of Cancer.

15. Which of the following is an example of checks and balances in the United States government?

   A. the fact that you must be 18 years of age to vote
   B. the first amendment of the Constitution
   C. the Louisiana Purchase
   D. the fact that the president can veto a law that Congress passes

16. The name of the shelter that the Hodenosaunee (Iroquois) constructed for several families to live in is

   A. a pueblo.   **C.** a palisade.
   B. a teepee.   **D.** a longhouse.

17. Which of the following is not an example of how the Hodenosaunee (Iroquois) used their environment to meet their needs or wants?

   A. Deerskin was used to make clothing.
   B. Headdresses were decorated with eagle feathers.
   C. Canoes were made from trees.
   D. Women were the head of the family structure.

Please use the following map to answer Questions 18–20.

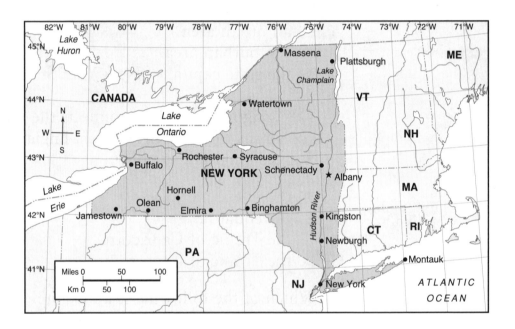

18. In order to drive from Buffalo to Syracuse, what city would you most likely pass through?

   A. Binghamton
   B. New York City
   C. Rochester
   D. Albany

19. The distance from Buffalo to Syracuse is

    A. less than 50 miles.
    B. more than 50 miles.
    C. about 50 miles.

20. Which Great Lake forms part of New York State's western border?

    A. Lake Erie
    B. Lake Ontario
    C. Atlantic Ocean
    D. Lake Champlain

21. Money that people pay to their government to help pay for services in the community is called

    A. income.
    B. checks and balances.
    C. taxes.
    D. goods and services.

Base your answer to Question 22 on the following partial outline:

I._____
     A. Legislative
     B. Judicial
     C. Executive

22. Which heading belongs after Roman numeral I?

    A. Laws
    B. Parts of the Declaration of Independence
    C. Branches of United States and New York State Government
    D. Continents

23. Two hundred years ago, people in different regions of the world probably ate different types of foods because

    A. they were able to grow and hunt different foods based on their environment.
    B. they just didn't like the same things.
    C. they couldn't all afford the same things.
    D. they could only grow corn.

24. Matthew earns $6 per hour for his job at the golf course. This money is called his

    A. income.
    B. expenses.
    C. taxes.
    D. allowance.

25. Ian decides to spend his birthday money on a beautiful new atlas. Is he using his money to purchase a need or a want?

    A. a need
    B. a want

26. Which list shows these events in the order that they happened, from the earliest to the most recent?

    A. New York was established.—New Netherland was established.—The United States was established.
    B. The United States was established.—New Netherland was established.—New York was established.
    C. New Netherland was established.—The United States was established.—New York was established.
    D. New Netherland was established.—New York was established.—The United States was established.

Please answer Questions 27 and 28 using the following chart.

Year	Event
1848	First Women's Rights Convention is held in Seneca Falls, New York.
1866	The American Equal Rights Association is formed to support women's rights.
1869	Women are given the right to vote in the territory of Wyoming.
1917	Jeannette Rankin of Montana becomes the first woman elected to Congress.
1920	The 19th Amendment to the Constitution is approved. It gives women the right to vote.
1920	League of Women Voters is formed to educate women voters about the issues.

27. In what year did the first woman get elected to Congress?

    A. 1848
    B. 1920
    C. 1862
    D. 1917

28. How many years were there between women getting the right to vote in the territory of Wyoming and women getting the right to vote in the whole United States when the 19th Amendment was passed?
    A. 20 years
    B. 54 years
    C. 51 years
    D. 42 years

29. Which of the following lists contains only the names of continents?

    A. Canada, Europe, Asia, New Zealand
    B. Italy, North America, South America, China
    C. New York, Montana, Maine, Maryland
    D. North America, South America, Europe, Asia

30. Which type of government do we have in the United States?

    A. a democracy
    B. a monarchy
    C. a dictatorship
    D. no government

31. One reason that immigrants might have come to the United States is

    A. to have freedom of religion.
    B. to find a good job and earn money.
    C. to escape war in their own country.
    D. all of the above.

32. The United States is a producer of automobiles. These automobiles are sold in Canada. Canada is a producer of lumber. This lumber is then sold in the United States. This is an example of how the economies of Canada and the United States are

    A. independent.
    B. democratic.
    C. interdependent.
    D. transatlantic.

33. It costs a store $6 to make a sweatshirt, and they sell it for $35. The amount of profit that the store will make is

A. $29.
B. $35.
C. $41.
D. $6.

34. One reason that the colonists fought the Revolutionary War against Great Britain is that

A. they wanted to become a colony of France.
B. they were being heavily taxed without being represented in the British government—"taxation without representation."
C. they were angry because the British dumped the colonists' tea into Boston Harbor during the Boston Tea Party.
D. they wanted to return to Britain, and the British wouldn't let them.

35. Which of the following is not a way that we show pride in our country?

A. flying our flag
B. saying the Pledge of Allegiance
C. going on vacation in Europe
D. celebrating Independence Day on the Fourth of July

CONSTRUCTED RESPONSE QUESTIONS

1. Please use the chart below to answer Questions 1–3.

Area (in Square Miles) of the Great Lakes

Name of the Lake	Area in Square Miles
Lake Erie	32,630
Lake Huron	74,700
Lake Superior	81,000
Lake Ontario	34,850
Lake Michigan	67,900

1. Which of the Great Lakes has the largest area in square miles?

_____

_____

2. Which of the Great Lakes has a smaller area than Lake Ontario?

_____

_____

3. Which two of the Great Lakes share a border with New York State?

_____

_____

2. Please use the cartoon below to answer Questions 1–3.

1. What is the job of the man shown in the cartoon?

_____

2. According to this cartoon, what is one of the duties of the president of the United States?

_____

3. The duties on this man's hats do not represent all the jobs in running a country. Why doesn't the president of the United States have all the powers and duties of government?

_____
_____
_____

3. Please use the circle graphs below to answer Questions 1–3.

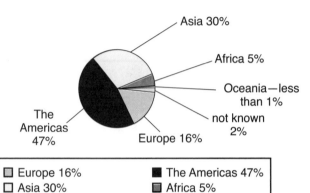

Immigration by Region 1820

Europe 92%

The Americas 5%

Asia—less than 1%

Africa—less than 1%

Oceania—less than 1%

not known 3%

- ☐ Europe 92%   ■ The Americas 5%
- ☐ Asia—less than 1%   ◼ Africa—less than 1%
- ☐ Oceania—less than 1%   ☐ not known 3%

Immigration by Region 2000

Asia 30%

Africa 5%

Oceania—less than 1%

not known 2%

The Americas 47%

Europe 16%

- ☐ Europe 16%   ■ The Americas 47%
- ☐ Asia 30%   ◼ Africa 5%
- ☐ Oceania—less than 1%   ☐ not known 2%

1. From which region of the world did the most immigrants come in 1820?

_____

_____

2. Did the percentage of immigrants from Africa increase, decrease, or stay the same from 1820 to 2000?

_____

_____

3. Name one country that an immigrant from Europe might be from.

_____

_____

4. Please use the diagram below to answer Questions 1–3.

**Succession for the Office of the President
of the United States of America**

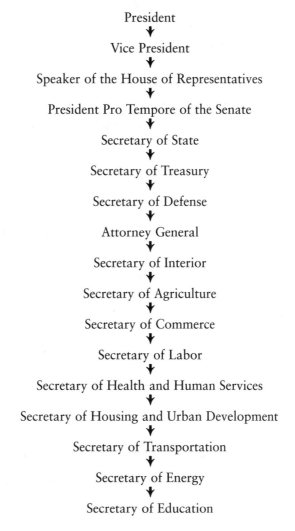

President
↓
Vice President
↓
Speaker of the House of Representatives
↓
President Pro Tempore of the Senate
↓
Secretary of State
↓
Secretary of Treasury
↓
Secretary of Defense
↓
Attorney General
↓
Secretary of Interior
↓
Secretary of Agriculture
↓
Secretary of Commerce
↓
Secretary of Labor
↓
Secretary of Health and Human Services
↓
Secretary of Housing and Urban Development
↓
Secretary of Transportation
↓
Secretary of Energy
↓
Secretary of Education

1. Who is the next in line for becoming president after the attorney general?

_____

2. How many people would become president before the secretary of education would, if something were to happen to the president?

_____

3. Which branch of government does the president head?

_____

DOCUMENT-BASED ESSAY QUESTION

Directions: The following task is based on Documents 1–5. This question is designed to test your ability to work with historical documents. Look at each document and answer the questions that follow. Use the answers to these questions to help you write your essay.

Historical background: The people of the world have always developed their culture by using those things found in their environment to help them meet their needs and wants.

Task:

For Part A, read each document carefully and answer the question or questions that follow. Then read the directions for Part B and write your essay.

For Part B, use the information from the documents, your answers to Part A, and your knowledge of social studies to write a well-organized essay. In your essay, you should:

Tell how the people of the different regions of the world have used those things found in their environment to help them meet their needs and wants.

PART A: SHORT-ANSWER QUESTIONS

Directions: Read each document and answer the question or questions that follow each document in the space provided.

Document 1

As the season turns toward winter in New York State, people's thoughts start to turn toward winter recreation. There are many fabulous skiing resorts across New York State. Families look forward to great days of exciting skiing in beautiful countryside. In addition to the downhill skiing resorts, there are miles and miles of cross-country skiing trails that meander through New York's scenic parks. These trails are great for hiking too! And for those of us that truly like to remain young at heart, you can never outgrow a steep sledding hill! New York comes alive when the snow hits the ground!

1. According to this passage, what are two things that people in New York State can do for entertainment in the winter?

(a) _____

(b) _____

Document 2

Items Grown and Exported from the Amazon Rain Forest
Mango Fruit
Brazil Nuts
Rosewood Oil
Quinine Bark (used in medicines)
Cashew Nuts
Natural Rubber

1. Name two products that are exported from the Amazon rain forest.

_____

_____

Document 3

1. Based on this picture, name one way that the people living in this polar region of the world have used their environment to help them meet their needs or wants.

_____

Document 4

This man is not fishing for fun: fishing is his job.

1. How do people who fish for a living make money from fishing?

_____

_____

_____

_____

_____

Document 5

1. How have the people that live here used things that are found in their environment to help them meet their need for transportation?

_____

_____

_____

_____

_____

PART B: ESSAY

Directions: The following task is based on Documents 1–5. This question is designed to test your ability to work with historical documents. Look at each document and answer the questions that follow. Use the answers to these questions to help you write your essay.

Historical background: The people of the world have always developed their culture by using those things found in their environment to help them meet their needs and wants.

Task:

For Part A, read each document and answer the question or questions that follow it carefully. Then read the directions for Part B and write your essay.

For Part B, use the information from the documents, your answers to Part A, and your knowledge of social studies to write a well-organized essay. In your essay, you should:

> Tell how the people of the different regions of the world have used those things found in their environment to help them meet their needs and wants.

Planning Page

Use this page to help you to plan for your essay. Work that you do on this page will *not* count toward your final grade. Do not write your essay here.

Use the following space to write your essay.

Another Complete Practice Test

Now it is time to try out all of the strategies and hints that you have learned. You will have 90 minutes to complete the multiple-choice and constructed response questions. You will then have another 90 minutes to do the document-based essay question.

PRACTICE TEST 2

MULTIPLE-CHOICE QUESTIONS

Directions: Please use your knowledge of social studies to choose the best answer to each of the following questions.

1. Which of the following is an example of a primary source?

   A. a newly released movie about World War II
   B. a diary entry written by a soldier during the Civil War
   C. a social studies textbook
   D. a Web site that tells about the life of Christopher Columbus

2. What do the stars on the American flag represent?

   A. the 50 states
   B. the original colonies
   C. the number of explorers who explored the new world
   D. the age of our current president

Use the following chart to answer Questions 3–5.

Average Size of Farms in America (in Acres)

Year	Number of Acres
1940	174
1950	213
1960	297
1970	374
1980	426
1999	432

3. During what year shown on the chart was the average American farm the smallest?

   A. 1999
   B. 1970
   C. 1910
   D. 1940

4. During which decade did the size of the average farm increase from 374 acres to 426 acres?

   A. 1920–1930
   B. 1970–1980
   C. 1940–1960
   D. 1960–1970

5. The farms shown in the graph are most likely located in

   A. rural areas.
   B. urban areas.
   C. suburban areas.
   D. Canada.

6. What is the introduction to the Constitution of the United States of America called? It explains why the Constitution was written.

    A. the executive branch
    B. the amendments
    C. the articles
    D. the Preamble

7. Which of the following freedoms is not guaranteed by the Bill of Rights?

    A. speech
    B. press
    C. religion
    D. medicine

8. Which of the following is an example of scarcity?

    A. There are enough apples for everyone to eat.
    B. Lyn earns $15 an hour for her job as head gardener.
    C. Owen has $20 more than Graham in his savings account.
    D. The toy store had 30 copies of a popular new video game, and 50 people were waiting in line to buy it.

Use the following graph to answer Questions 9–11.

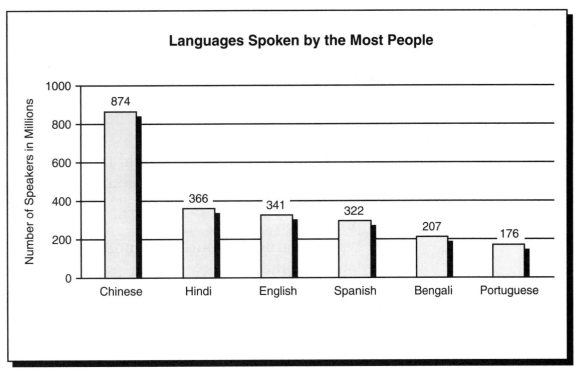

9. Which language is spoken by 176 million people in the world?

   A. Hindi   **C.** English
   B. Portuguese   **D.** French

10. How many more people speak Chinese than English in the world?

   A. 533 million people
   B. 1,215 million people
   C. 543 million people
   D. You cannot tell from this graph.

11. The most common language in the world is Chinese. Most of the people who speak this language live on which continent?

   A. Australia   **C.** Asia
   B. North America   **D.** Antarctica

12. The Supreme Court is made up of members of which branch of the United States government?

    A. preamble
    B. executive
    C. judicial
    D. legislative

13. Which of the following factors would influence the climate of a country?

    A. the population
    B. the type of natural resources found there
    C. the language they speak
    D. their distance from the equator

14. Which of the following statements is true about natural resources?

    A. They are produced by human beings.
    B. They are not used in the United States.
    C. Some are nonrenewable.
    D. None can be found in New York State.

15. Which of the following lakes can be found in New York State?

    A. Lake Erie
    B. Lake Champlain
    C. Lake Ontario
    D. All of the above.

Use the following timeline to answer Questions 16 and 17.

Selected States and When They Became States

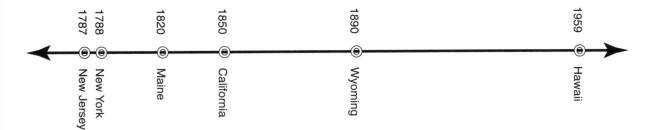

16. Which of the states shown became a state in 1890?

    A. Wyoming   **C.** Texas
    B. New York   **D.** Maine

17. Which of the following statements is true?

    A. Wyoming became a state before California.
    B. New York became a state after California.
    C. California and Maine became states in the same year.
    D. New York became a state before Maine.

18. What is the name of the document that was approved on July 4, 1776, and sent to Great Britain?

    A. the Constitution
    B. the State of the Union Address
    C. the Bill of Rights
    D. the Declaration of Independence

19. New York State produces apples and corn and sells them to Florida. Florida produces oranges and sells them to New York State. This is an example of

    A. independence.   **C.** scarcity.
    B. interdependence.   **D.** primary source material.

20. Which of the following Native American tribes settled in New York State?

    A. the Sioux
    B. the Pueblo
    C. the Mohawk
    D. the Inuit

21. What is the name of the country that shares a border with New York State?

    A. Canada
    B. Mexico
    C. Vermont
    D. Lake Ontario

22. Which of the following is an example of an expense that a family might have?

    A. doing homework
    B. buying groceries
    C. playing checkers together
    D. making their own beds

23. Which of the following is a fact about the United States government?

    A. Congress is made up of the Senate and the House of Representatives.
    B. If you do not vote, you are a bad citizen.
    C. The government should spend more money on education.
    D. Franklin Delano Roosevelt was the best president we have ever had.

24. I._____
    A. food
    B. water
    C. shelter

Which is the best heading to put in the blank in this outline?

A. Basic Human Wants   C. Cultures
B. Customs   D. Basic Human Needs

25. Which of the following is not a reason that the colonists declared their independence from Great Britain?

    A. Britain put taxes on many items.
    B. Britain did not include colonists in the decisions that the government was making.
    C. They wanted to break apart and make 13 new countries.
    D. They wanted to form a new government, which would be controlled by the people.

26. A person who agrees to work for someone else for a set period of time in exchange for their ticket to the new world was called

    A. a slave.   C. a loyalist.
    B. a colonist.   D. an indentured servant.

27. Native Americans

    A. only took what they needed from nature.
    B. polluted rivers and streams with factories.
    C. wasted parts of the animals that they hunted by not using them.
    D. believed that they could take anything that they wanted from the earth and didn't have to give anything back.

28. One way that we can participate in our government is by

    A. running for a position in the government.
    B. voting on election day.
    C. writing a letter to our state senator that tells our opinions about an issue.
    D. All of the above.

29. If you were planning a trip to your Grandma's and Grandpa's house near Rochester, New York, which type of map would you use to help you get there?

    A. a physical map
    B. a historical map
    C. a road map
    D. a political map of the eastern hemisphere of the world

30. Income is

    A. a person who moves to another country to live.
    B. the money that people pay to the government to pay for services in the community.
    C. things that your family has to buy such as food, clothes, and cars.
    D. the money that you earn from a job.

31. As you travel farther away from the equator, the temperature

    A. gets warmer.
    B. gets colder.
    C. stays the same.
    D. All of the above.

Base your answers to Questions 32 and 33 on the following chart.

Name of the State	Population in 1990	Population in 1999
Maine	1,227,928	1,253,040
Texas	16,986,335	20,044,141
New York	17,990,778	18,196,601
Connecticut	3,287,116	3,282,031
Georgia	6,478,149	7,788,240

32. Which state had a population of 20,044,141 in 1999?

A. Texas
B. Maine
C. Georgia
D. New York

33. Which state had a decrease in population from 1990 to 1999?

A. Texas
B. Connecticut
C. New York
D. Maine

34. Which of the following correctly describes the location of the United States?

A. It is in the northern and eastern hemispheres.
B. It is in the northern and southern hemispheres.
C. It is in the southern and western hemispheres.
D. It is in the northern and western hemispheres.

35. Scott earns $20 dollars for doing yard work. He has a plan for his money. He decides to spend $10 going to the movies with his friends. He pays his sister the $3 he owes her. He puts the remaining $7 into his savings account. Scott's plan for his money is called

A. a tax.
B. an income.
C. a budget.
D. an expense.

CONSTRUCTED RESPONSE QUESTIONS

1. Please use the chart below to answer Questions 1–3.

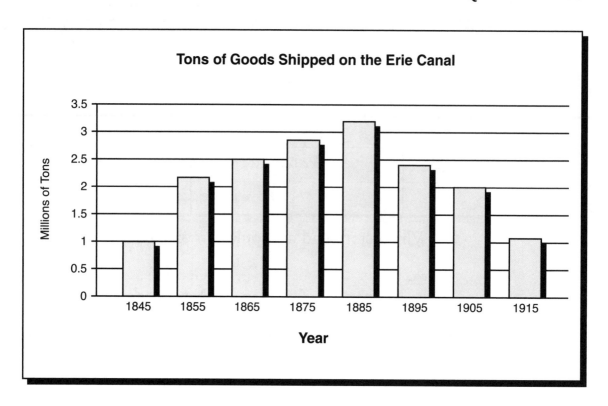

Tons of Goods Shipped on the Erie Canal

1. About how many tons of goods were shipped on the Erie Canal in 1895?

2. During which decade did the amount of goods shipped on the Erie Canal increase by more than one million tons?

3. What is one way that the Erie Canal helped New York State businesses?

2. Please use the table below to answer Questions 1–3.

Qualifications for President and Vice President of the United States of America

Office	Minimum Age	Citizenship	Residence	Limit of Terms	Length of Term
President of the United States of America	35	Born in the United States	Must have lived in the United States for at least 14 years	2 terms	4 years
Vice President of the United States of America	35	Born in the United States	Must have lived in the United States for at least 14 years	No limit	4 years

1. What is the youngest that a president of the United States of America could be?

   _____

2. How many years could a person serve as president?

   _____

3. Which branch of the United States government is the president the head of?

   _____

3. Please use the table below to answer Questions 1–3.

Average January Temperature for Selected Cities

Name of the City	Average January Temperature (in °F)
Buffalo, New York	24°F
Charleston, South Carolina	48°F
Fairbanks, Alaska	–13°F
Hartford, Connecticut	25°F
Miami, Florida	67°F
New York, New York	32°F
Portland, Maine	22°F

1. Which city, shown on the table, has an average temperature of about 32°F for the month of January?

_____

2. Which is the only city on the table that has an average temperature of below 0°F for the month of January?

_____

3. Why does the city in Alaska have a much colder average temperature than the city in Florida?

_____

_____

_____

_____

4. Please use the table below to answer Questions 1–3.

Voter Turnout During Presidential Election Years

Year	% Of Eligible Voters Who Voted
1960	63
1964	62
1968	61
1972	55
1976	54
1980	53
1984	53
1988	50
1992	55
1996	49

1. What percentage of eligible voters voted in the 1976 election?

_____

2. Which is the only year during which the percentage of eligible voters voting increased from the previous presidential election?

_____

3. Why is voting an important thing to do?

_____

_____

_____

DOCUMENT-BASED ESSAY QUESTION

Directions: The following task is based on Documents 1–5. This question is designed to test your ability to work with historical documents. Look at each document and answer the questions that follow. Use the answers to these questions to help you write your essay.

Historical background: The world is constantly changing. Improvements in transportation, communication, and manufacturing are always being made. America changed a great deal during the 1800s. Technological changes are mainly responsible for these changes.

Task

For Part A, read each document carefully and answer the question or questions that follow. Then read the directions for Part B and write your essay.

For Part B, use the information from the documents, your answers to Part A, and your knowledge of social studies to write a well-organized essay. In your essay, you should:

> Explain at least three ways that communities in America have changed because of improvements in technology.

PART A: SHORT-ANSWER QUESTIONS

Directions: *Read each document carefully and answer the question or questions that follow each document in the space provided.*

Document 1

Orville and Wilbur Wright's test of the Wright Model Airplane

1. The Wright brothers are famous for which successful invention, shown in this picture?

_____

Document 2

Inventions in Communication

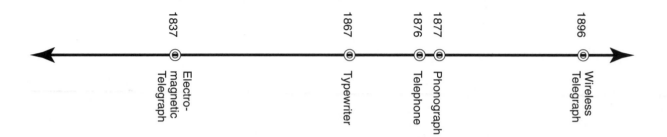

1837 Electro-magnetic Telegraph

1867 Typewriter

1876 Telephone

1877 Phonograph

1896 Wireless Telegraph

1. List two inventions in communication that were made during the 1800s.

(a) _____

(b) _____

Document 3

Railroads Across America

Growth in the railroad industry in America exploded during the 1800s. The first charter for a railroad was granted in 1815. By 1829, the first steam locomotive had taken its first trip in the United States. After that, tracks were quickly put up across the country. In 1850, there were 9,000 miles of track. By 1860, this number was over 30,000 miles. Then by 1870, there were a whopping 53,000 miles of railroad track. By that time, there were also "sleeping cars" and a transcontinental railroad. This made it possible to travel from the Atlantic Coast to the Pacific Coast in comfort. This railroad growth changed our country forever.

1. How many more miles of railroad tracks were there in America in 1870 than in 1850?

_____

_____

_____

Document 4

Year	Total U.S. Population	% Living in Urban Areas	% Living in Rural Areas
1790	3,929,214	5.1	94.9
1830	12,860,702	8.8	91.2
1870	38,558,371	25.7	74.3
1910	92,228,496	45.6	54.4
1950	151,325,798	59.6	40.4
1990	248,709,873	75.2	24.8

1. Did the percentage (%) of Americans living in urban areas increase or decrease from 1790 to 1990?

_____

_____

Document 5

The Model T Ford

Henry Ford, of the Ford Motor Company, wanted to make a car that all people could afford to buy. He designed the Model T Ford. He wanted to make it quickly and cheaply, so he began to use a moving assembly line. This meant that the car would move from worker to worker on the assembly line. Each worker was very good and very fast at doing his or her part to build the car. Then the car moved onto the next person. This improvement in production allowed Ford to lower his prices. It also made the Model T Ford one of the most famous cars in history.

Prices for a Model T Ford:

1909: $950
1916: $360
1926: $290

1. How was Henry Ford able to make his cars cheaper and faster?

_____

_____

_____

_____

_____

_____

PART B: ESSAY

Directions: The following task is based on Documents 1–5. This question is designed to test your ability to work with historical documents. Look at each document and answer the questions that follow. Use the answers to these questions to help you write your essay.

Historical background: The world is constantly changing. Improvements in transportation, communication, and manufacturing are always being made. America changed a great deal during the 1800s. Technological changes are mainly responsible for these changes.

Task

For Part B, use the information from the documents, your answers to part A, and your knowledge of social studies to write a well-organized essay. In your essay, you should:

> Explain at least three ways that communities in America have changed because of improvements in technology.

Planning Page

Use this page to help you plan for your essay. Work that you do on this page will *not* count toward your final grade. Do not write your essay here.

Use the following space to write your essay.

Practice Test 1—Answer Key

Let's check your answers and see how you did.

MULTIPLE-CHOICE QUESTIONS

1. *Answer:* C

Explanation: Be careful that you read questions carefully! This question asks which of the following people did *not* explore in New York. Christopher Columbus is the only explorer listed who did not explore in New York State.

2. *Answer:* A

Explanation: Natural resources are things that are found naturally in or on the earth and can be used by humans. Trees can be used for many things from lumber to paper-making, lakes are a resource for transportation benefits and fishing. Coal is found in the earth and is used as a fuel. Therefore A is the correct answer. All the other choices contain something that has been made by humans and cannot be considered a natural resource.

3. *Answer:* B

Explanation: In this question, you can eliminate Choice C because Normandy was a battle during World War II, not the Revolutionary War. Choice D, the Battle of Lexington, was the first battle of the Revolutionary War and Choice A, the Battle of Yorktown, was the last battle of the Revolutionary War. The Battle of Saratoga (1877) is commonly known as the turning point of the war.

4. *Answer:* C

Explanation: This question is testing whether or not you know the difference between a fact and an opinion. In this case, facts about rural areas include the statements that there may be farms, there are not many factories, and the population may be lower than in urban areas. This is a good question to remind you that you should always choose the *best* answer to a question. You may want to argue that it is an opinion that there are not many factories in rural areas. However, the best answer is Choice C, "Rural areas are beautiful." This is clearly somebody's opinion about what is beautiful. Sometimes kids try to prove that another answer is right, but you must choose the best answer, definitely C!

5. *Answer:* C

Explanation: This question measures whether or not you are able to read information from a timeline. To find the answer, you can start at the earliest date on the far left of the timeline and read the events until you find one that is one of the choices to answer to this question. Actually, the first item listed on the timeline is the correct answer, bifocal lenses.

6. *Answer:* A

Explanation: To answer this question, you must remember that the Declaration of Independence was approved on July 4, 1776. This timeline does not start until 1784; therefore, all the events happened after the Declaration of Independence was approved.

7. *Answer:* D

Explanation: This question is testing whether you understand the difference between goods and services. Goods are actual things that are produced in an area. Services are the things that people do to help people meet their needs and wants. Furniture, cars, and clothing are all goods that a community produces and can export or sell to other communities. Since the question asks which is not a good, the answer is Choice D, firefighters; they provide a service.

8. *Answer:* A

Explanation: You can eliminate Choices B and D because they were craftspeople. A cooper makes barrels and a blacksmith makes things from iron. That leaves a patriot or a loyalist as your most reasonable answers. You will need to remember that a patriot wanted freedom from the British and a loyalist stayed loyal to the King of England. A helpful hint is that the word "loyalist" has the word "loyal" in it!

9. *Answer:* B

Explanation: To answer this question, you must read the chart about national parks. It is helpful to read down through the Interesting Feature column until you find the description that says the park contains the highest mountain in the United States. This is found in the third row down. Then read across that row to the State column and find that Alaska is the correct answer.

10. *Answer:* A

Explanation: You will need to follow a few steps in order to answer this question. First of all, you need to know where Yosemite National Park is. You can use the chart about national parks to find this information. You will find that it is in California. Then you must use your knowledge of geography to help you. You should know that California is a state on the west coast of the United States. New York is in the east. To travel from the east to the west coast, you must travel west, Choice A.

11. *Answer:* D

Explanation: This question tests your understanding of the New York colony. Both farming and being a craftsperson are jobs that a colonist might have, so Choice D, all of the above, is the correct answer.

12. *Answer:* D

Explanation: This question tests your knowledge of our national holidays. We celebrate D, Martin Luther King, Jr. Day, on his birthday in January to honor his work for civil rights.

13. *Answer:* B

Explanation: Many of you may automatically know that B is the right answer, especially if you live there! However, you can use clues in this question to help you choose the correct answer. You can eliminate D because, as you know, Albany is our state capital. Now you need to remember the definitions of rural, urban, and suburban areas. Part of the definition of an urban area is that it is often called a city. New York City has the word "city" right in its name; therefore, it must be an urban area.

14. *Answer:* A

Explanation: This question is really a definition question. All the answers listed are the names of lines of latitude, except the prime meridian. Choice A is the correct answer. This question should remind you how important it is to review the definitions of the words found in the vocabulary section of this book, Appendix A. It is really a great way to prepare.

15. *Answer:* D

Explanation: Checks and balances are the way that the three branches of our government are interconnected and can check up on each other. You can eliminate the Louisiana Purchase because it is the name of a land purchase, which is not related to how the government works. Both Choices A and B are related to our government, but they are not examples of how the branches check up on each other. Answer D is correct because the president (executive branch) can check on Congress (legislative branch) by vetoing a law that it makes.

16. *Answer:* D

Explanation: You will remember from learning about the Iroquois that the correct name for them is the Hodenosaunee. This name actually means "people of the longhouse" because they built longhouses as shelter.

17. *Answer:* D

Explanation: This question asks about how the Hodenosaunee used their environment to meet their needs and wants. The fact that women were the head of the family structure is true, but it is not related to meeting needs and wants found in the environment. Therefore, Choice D is the correct answer.

18. *Answer:* C

Explanation: Be sure to use the map that is given to help you with this question. Start by finding Buffalo and Syracuse, and then trace the route that you would most likely travel. As you do so, you should look to see what city you will pass through. It will be Rochester.

19. *Answer:* B

Explanation: In order to answer this question, you should use the scale of miles. It is not necessary to calculate an exact distance. Estimating will help you to determine whether the distance is greater than, less than, or equal to 50 miles. It is actually about 150 miles from Buffalo to Syracuse.

20. *Answer:* A

Explanation: Looking at the map of New York State and using the compass rose to help you find the western border of the state, you will see that Lake Erie forms part of that border.

21. *Answer:* C

Explanation: This question is another example of how important it is to learn social studies vocabulary. You can use the vocabulary section of this book in Appendix A as a study tool. The question gives the definition of the word "taxes."

22. *Answer:* C

Explanation: This question gives you a partial outline. In this case, they have given you three items, and you need to choose a heading that explains what they are. Our country's government divides the powers of government between three branches: executive, judicial, and legislative. The correct answer is Choice C.

23. *Answer:* A

Explanation: The best answer for this question is Choice A. While some of the other choices may be true, such as they didn't know about other foods, the best answer is A. What people eat is usually based on what they can grow and what they can hunt based on their environment.

24. *Answer:* A

Explanation: Money that you earn from a job is called your income. I like to remember it by thinking that it is the money that "comes in" to your wallet . . . income!

25. *Answer:* B

Explanation: Although an atlas is a great thing to spend your money on, it is not a need because you would not die if you didn't have it. It is a want.

26. *Answer:* D

Explanation: This question asks you to list the three given events in the order that they happened. When you first look at this type of question, it can be confusing. A strategy that works well is to start with Choice A and to read it from the beginning to the end to see if the events are in order. When you do this, you will notice that New York was not formed before New Netherland. Therefore, Choice A is incorrect. Follow this plan for the rest of the choices. Choice D puts the three events in the right order.

27. *Answer:* D

Explanation: To answer this question, you must read the chart carefully. Read through the event descriptions until you find the one that lists Jeannette Rankin of Montana becoming the first woman elected to Congress. Then look back to find that it was in the year 1917.

28. *Answer:* C

Explanation: This question will require you to use a little math to calculate the answer. The first step is to find out when women were given the right to vote in Wyoming. Use the chart to find that it was in 1869. Then find the date that women were given the right to vote in the whole United States, with the 19th Amendment. It was in 1920. In order to find out how many years were between the two dates, you need to subtract.

$$
\begin{array}{r}
1920 \\
-\ 1869 \\
\hline
51\ \text{years}
\end{array}
$$

29. *Answer:* D

Explanation: You will remember learning about the seven continents of the world. This question asks you to read each list and to find the one that contains only continent names. This may be tricky because some of them may contain the names of continents and countries. But remember that you want to choose the one that lists *only* continents. Choice A lists two continents, but Canada and New Zealand are the names of countries. Choice B also lists two continents but China and Italy are also the names of countries. Choice C lists four states. Only Choice D lists all continents.

30. *Answer:* A

Explanation: There are many types of government in the world. The type or style of government that we have in our country is called a democracy.

31. *Answer:* D

Explanation: Throughout America's history there have been hundreds of thousands of immigrants. There is no one reason why all people come to America. All of the answers given are reasonable answers.

32. *Answer:* C

Explanation: The definition of interdependent is: the way in which communities depend on each other to help meet their needs and wants. This question is a good example of this concept.

33. *Answer:* A

Explanation: Profit is the amount of money that a company actually makes when they sell a product. To calculate profit, you must subtract the cost to make the item from the amount it is sold for: $35 − $6 = $29 profit.

34. *Answer:* B

Explanation: The phrase "taxation without representation" is a common phrase used to describe colonial motives for the Revolutionary War. All of the other answers are inaccurate and, therefore, incorrect.

35. *Answer:* C

Explanation: When we show our pride in our country, we are showing respect for an event or a symbol of our country. Going to Europe is not an example of this.

CONSTRUCTED RESPONSE QUESTIONS

Constructed Response Question 1

1. *Answer:* Lake Superior

Explanation: To answer this question, look carefully at the chart about the Great Lakes. The second column lists the area of the lakes in square miles. The largest number in this column is 81,000. It is the amount of square miles for Lake Superior, which means that it is the largest.

2. *Answer:* Lake Erie

Explanation: There are really two steps to this problem. The first is to find the area of Lake Ontario. Read down the column labeled Name of the Lake until you find Lake Ontario; then, read across to find the area. It is

34,850 square miles. After you have done this, look through the Area in Square Miles column to find numbers smaller than 34,850. The only one that you will find is 32,630. As you read across you will see that this is the area of Lake Erie. Therefore, Lake Erie has a smaller area in square miles than Lake Ontario and is the correct answer.

3. *Answer:* Lake Erie and Lake Ontario

Explanation: As the third question in a constructed response question, you will remember that this is the question where you may have to bring in some outside knowledge. In this case, you will need your knowledge of New York State's geography. Two of the Great Lakes form borders for New York State; they are Lake Erie and Lake Ontario. However, this question is a great example of how you can use your thinking skills and help yourself to get the correct answer. You might remember that Questions 18–20 in the multiple-choice section were related to a map of New York State. Since this map is in the same portion of the test, you can look back at it and get the information that you need to answer this question correctly. Pretty clever!

Constructed Response Question 2

1. *Answer:* President

Explanation: The man in the cartoon is wearing a large button that says "President." If you were confused and thought that maybe the hats were the names of this man's job, hopefully you were able to correct this answer when you got to Question 3 and were told that the hats represented duties.

2. *Answer:* Any one of the following is correct: Law Executer, Nation Leader, Party Leader, Commander in Chief, or World Leader.

Explanation: The hats that the man is wearing represent the powers or duties that he has as the president of the United States.

3. *Answer/Explanation:* Your answer should explain that our country is set up to have three branches of government. Also that the powers are shared among those three branches to make sure that one person does not have all of the power. If you want to add that this is because we did not want to create a government similar to the one in England, that would be great extra information.

Constructed Response Question 3

1. *Answer:* Europe
Explanation: Look at the circle graph for 1820. The largest piece is labeled "Europe."

2. *Answer:* Increase
Explanation: The percentage of immigrants from Africa in 1820 was less than 1 percent. By 2000 the percentage had gone up to 5 percent. This is an increase.

3. *Answer/Explanation:* There are several answers to this question; not all can be included here. You must have named a country in the continent of Europe. Several examples include England, France, Germany, Italy, Spain, Portugal, Switzerland, Poland, Denmark, Belgium, The Netherlands, Sweden, Norway, and Finland. Check with a grown-up or a map to see if you answered correctly if your choice is not listed here.

Constructed Response Question 4

1. *Answer:* Secretary of the interior
Explanation: Look at the diagram that is shown. If you follow the arrows down you will see that after the attorney general is the secretary of the interior.

2. *Answer:* 15

Explanation: You need to count how many people come after the president but before the secretary of education. The vice president would be one and on through the secretary of energy, which makes fifteen. Do not count the secretary of education because the question asks how many are before the secretary of education.

3. *Answer:* Executive

Explanation: This question tests your outside knowledge of the government. Remember that our government is set up in three branches: the executive, legislative, and judicial. The president heads the executive branch.

DOCUMENT-BASED SCAFFOLDING QUESTIONS

Document 1

1. *Answer:* Any two of the following are acceptable answers: downhill skiing, cross-country skiing, sledding, or hiking.

Explanation: This article discusses different things that people do in New York for recreation. All the activities listed use the natural surroundings and climate of New York to provide recreation.

Document 2

1. *Answer:* Any two of the following are acceptable answers: mango fruit, brazil nuts, rosewood oil, quinine bark, cashew nuts, or natural rubber.

Explanation: These items are all grown and produced in the Amazon rain forest. Due to the soil and climate, these items are available in the environment. They are then exported. This means that these items are sold to other countries for money. The people of the Amazon rain forest can then use that money to buy different things that they need or want.

Document 3

1. *Answer/Explanation:* The answer is that the people living in this polar region of the world have used the snow found in their environment to meet their need for shelter. The shelter is called an igloo and is made from snow and ice. Although there are other ways that people in polar regions use their environment, this is the only acceptable answer. This is because the question says, "Based on this picture . . ." Be careful!

Document 4

1. *Answer/Explanation:* This question asks you to explain how people who fish make a living at fishing. To answer this question, you must explain that these workers go fishing each day to catch fish. They then sell these fish to stores, restaurants, and other people. In return they get money, which they can use to purchase things that they need or want. They are using the natural resources of water and fish to provide a way to earn income.

Document 5

1. *Answer/Explanation:* The people in the picture are using the camels found in their environment to meet their need for transportation. Camels make excellent desert transportation because they are able to survive for long periods of time on little water.

DBQ SAMPLE ESSAY

Let's look at a few reminders about constructing your essay, before we look at a sample. You will need to read and re-read the question until you have a clear understanding of the question you need to write about. In this question, you are asked to write about how people from all over the world have used things in their environment to help them meet their needs and wants. It is important to recognize that there are two ways to do this. One is to grow or produce things for your own use. The other choice is to grow or produce things that can be sold to others for money. This money can then help you buy other things you need or want.

Sample Essay

All the people in the world need the same things to survive. We need food, water, shelter, and possibly clothing, depending on the climate we live in. Many people of the world have similar wants, including some form of recreation, transportation, education, and ways to earn money. However, all over the world people's cultures are very different. In other words, the way we meet those needs and wants is different. This is probably because people use those things found in their environment to help them meet their needs and wants. They do this in many ways.

People often use their environment to help them find the food that they need. One example of this is the people of the tropical Amazon rain forest. They are able to grow foods such as mango fruits, cashew nuts, and brazil nuts. These are just a few of the foods that can grow in this region of the world. Another example of the way that our environment can provide food is through fishing. People who fish for a living are able to catch fish, which are a great source of nutrition. But food isn't the only need that we meet using our environment. Oftentimes people use things they can find locally to build their shelters. An excellent example of this is people living in polar regions; they can build shelters called igloos out of snow and ice. These shelters are a great protection against the cold climate. These are just a few of the ways that we use our environment to meet our needs.

We also use things from our environment to meet our wants. One example of this is to provide recreation. For example, the people that live in New York State can use the land and the snow during the winter for skiing, sledding, and hiking. People really enjoy these outdoor activities. Another want that people have is for good transportation. Depending on where you live, that transportation can be very different. In the desert, you might use a camel for transportation. This is a great choice because camels can survive for long periods of time on very little water. However, if you live in a polar region of the world, a better choice for transportation might be a dogsled. Dogsleds are able to travel over snow and ice and are an excellent choice for polar regions.

The final way that we use our environment to help us to meet our needs and wants is to use it to make money. For example, people who fish don't just fish to feed themselves. They are able to sell the fish that they catch to other people, restaurants, and stores. They then earn money that they can use to buy other things that they need or want. In the Amazon rain forest, people are able to grow and produce several items such as rosewood oil, natural rubber, fruits, and nuts. They are then able to sell these items to other countries and earn money. They use this money to buy needs and wants.

As you can see, even though people all over the world have the same needs and similar wants, cultures are very different. We all use what we can find, grow, or do in our environment to meet our needs and wants. This is what makes learning about the world so interesting.

This essay would earn a score of 4 out of 4 because it is well organized, detailed, and clear. It is interesting to notice that the essay uses the answers to several of the scaffolding questions directly in the essay answer. This is a great idea.

Chapter 10

Practice Test 2—Answer Key

Let's check your answers and see how you did.

MULTIPLE-CHOICE QUESTIONS

1. *Answer:* B

   Explanation: A primary source is something that is actually from a time period or a person that lived through an event. Examples of primary sources include photographs, letters, diaries, and artifacts. The other type of source is called a secondary source. That means that the information is secondhand; in other words, it is like a retelling of events. Examples include textbooks, movies, and encyclopedias. All of the choices except for B are secondary sources. A diary entry written by a Civil War soldier would be a primary source.

2. *Answer:* A

   Explanation: There is one star on the flag for every state in our country. The stripes on the flag represent the thirteen original colonies. Our flag really shows how we began and who we are today. It is a true symbol of our country.

3. *Answer:* D

Explanation: If you read down through the column labeled Number of Acres, you can see that the smallest amount of acres that can be found is 174. Read over to the column labeled Year, and you will see that this was the average number of acres in the year 1940.

4. *Answer:* B

Explanation: Read down the Number of Acres column and find 374 acres. The next row down shows an increase to 426 acres. Reading over to the column labeled Year, you will see that these numbers are in the rows for the years 1970 and 1980.

5. *Answer:* A

Explanation: This question is checking your vocabulary. The definition of rural areas is that they may include many farms. Since this chart is about farms, it is really about rural areas.

6. *Answer:* D

Explanation: The Preamble to the Constitution is the introduction to it. A good clue is the prefix *pre-*. Whenever you see this prefix, it means before. The Preamble is before the rest of the Constitution; it is an introduction.

7. *Answer:* D

Explanation: All the other freedoms are guaranteed by the first 10 amendments of the Constitution, or Bill of Rights. Medicine is not mentioned anywhere.

8. *Answer:* D

Explanation: Scarcity means that the demand for something is greater than the supply. The situation described in D is an example of scarcity.

9. *Answer:* B

Explanation: Look carefully at the graph. Find the bar that is labeled 176 million speakers. It is the bar that represents Portuguese.

10. *Answer:* A

Explanation: Find the number of people that speak Chinese. It is 874,000,000 people. Then subtract the number of people that speak English, or 341,000,000 people. Set up the math problem in the following way:

$$\begin{array}{r} 874,000,000 \\ -\ 341,000,000 \\ \hline 533,000,000 \end{array}$$ more people speak Chinese than English

11. *Answer:* C

Explanation: To answer this question, you must remember what you learned about the continents in Grade 3. You will probably remember learning about Asia. China is a country in Asia. Most of the people who speak Chinese live in China, so C is the correct answer.

12. *Answer:* C

Explanation: The United States government is broken into three branches with different jobs. The executive branch, the legislative branch, and the judicial branch. The Supreme Court is at the head of the judicial branch.

13. *Answer:* D

Explanation: The farther away from the equator that an area is, the colder the climate. None of the other factors listed have any effect on the climate.

14. *Answer:* C

Explanation: Natural resources are things that come from the earth and can be used by humans to help us meet our needs and wants. There are two kinds of natural resources. One type is renewable, the kind that we can make more of, like trees and corn. The other type is called nonrenewable, which means we can't make more; when they are gone, they are gone. Examples include coal and oil. None of the other statements about resources is true.

15. *Answer:* D

Explanation: All of the lakes listed are in New York State. Lake Erie is on our state's western border. Lake Ontario is on our northern border. Lake Champlain is on our eastern border.

16. *Answer:* A

Explanation: Find the point on the timeline labeled 1890. It is labeled Wyoming.

17. *Answer:* D

Explanation: To answer this question, you will need to read each choice and check the facts it mentions to see if the statement is true. For example, A says that Wyoming became a state before California. You will need to find Wyoming on the timeline to see that it became a state in 1890. Then you need to check California. It became a state before Wyoming, in 1850. So A is not true. Check each of the choices this way until you realize that the only true statement is D.

18. *Answer:* D

Explanation: On July 4, 1776, the colonies approved the document that declared, or said, that they no longer wanted to be under British rule. In other words, they wanted to be independent. This document was called the Declaration of Independence. Its name really explains its purpose.

19. *Answer:* B

Explanation: Interdependence means the way in which communities depend on each other to meet their needs and wants. The people in Florida want corn and apples. These crops grow well in New York State so we sell them to Florida. The people of New York want oranges, which grow well in Florida. So New York State buys their oranges from Florida. The two states are interdependent.

20. *Answer:* C

Explanation: All the choices are names of Native American tribes, but only one of them is from New York. The Mohawk tribe is from New York.

21. *Answer:* A

Explanation: You can eliminate Choice C because it is not a country, it is a state. You can eliminate Choice D because it is a lake, not a country. The only two choices that are countries are Canada and Mexico. Mexico borders the United States on the southern border. Canada is the correct answer.

22. *Answer:* B

Explanation: Expenses are things that you must pay for. Every family has to buy groceries. They are an expense.

23. *Answer:* A

Explanation: Choices B, C, and D are all wrong because they are opinions about the government. Choice A is the only fact.

24. *Answer:* D

Explanation: All human beings need the same things to survive: food, water, and shelter.

25. *Answer:* C

Explanation: All the other choices are reasons that the colonists wanted their independence. Choice C is the correct answer because the colonists did not want to become 13 different countries.

26. *Answer:* D

Explanation: Many people came to the new world as indentured servants. Usually rich landowners would buy their ticket in exchange for several years worth of work once they arrived. For many, this was the only way they could afford to get to America.

27. *Answer:* A

Explanation: Native Americans have a deep appreciation for nature. They always try to give back to the earth when they use something. They do not waste things that they take from nature.

28. *Answer:* D

Explanation: The United States government is a democracy. This means that the people control the government and there are many ways to be a part of it. All the answers given are excellent ways to participate in government and decision making.

29. *Answer:* C

Explanation: Road maps are made especially for people traveling from one place to another. They show all of the roads and their names to help you to plan your route.

30. *Answer:* D

Explanation: The money that we earn from our jobs is called our income.

31. *Answer:* B

Explanation: Distance from the equator has a big impact on the climate of a place. The hottest places in the world are found right on the equator. The coldest places in the world are at the north and south poles, the farthest away from the equator that you can be.

32. *Answer:* A

Explanation: Look in the column that shows the population for 1999 and read down until you find the number 20,044,141. Look across the chart to see that it is in the row that represents Texas.

33. *Answer:* B

Explanation: Compare the populations for 1990 and 1999 for each state. The only state where the population number went down from 1990 to 1999 was Connecticut.

34. *Answer:* D

Explanation: Every location on earth is in either the eastern or western hemisphere. The United States is west of the prime meridian so it is in the western hemisphere. Every location on earth is in either the northern or southern hemisphere. The United States is north of the equator so it is in the northern hemisphere.

35. *Answer:* C

Explanation: A budget is a plan to organize how we spend or save the money that we earn.

CONSTRUCTED RESPONSE QUESTIONS

Constructed Response Question 1

1. *Answer:* About 2.4 millions of tons

Explanation: Find the bar labeled 1895 and follow it to the top. Then read across from the top to the scale on the left. You will see that the bar stops just before 2.5; therefore, it represents 2.4. The tricky part to this question is the labeling. What does the 2.4 mean? Read the label on the scale carefully to see that the numbers stand for the number of millions of tons. Be sure to label your answer that way. There is a very big difference between 2.4 tons and 2.4 million tons!

2. *Answer:* Between 1845 and 1855

Explanation: Notice that each line on the graph stands for 0.5 million tons. To find when the numbers increased by over one million tons, you will need to find a difference of at least two bars on the graph. This only happened between 1845 and 1855.

3. *Answer/Explanation:* To answer this question, you need to recall learning about the Erie Canal. There are several acceptable answers. They include:

• Businesses were able to ship goods faster.
• Businesses were able to ship goods cheaper.

- Businesses were able to sell to more people because they were able to ship their products farther.
- Businesses were able to make more money.

Constructed Response Question 2

1. *Answer:* 35 years old

Explanation: The chart shows the minimum age required to be president. Minimum means the least possible. The chart shows that the lowest possible age is 35 years old.

2. *Answer:* 8 years

Explanation: The president can only be elected president for two terms. Each term is 4 years long. $4 \times 2 = 8$ years.

3. *Answer:* Executive branch

Explanation: The United States government is divided into three branches of government: the executive, legislative, and judicial branches. The president is the head of the executive branch.

Constructed Response Question 3

1. *Answer:* New York, New York

Explanation: Find the number 32 in the column labeled Average January Temperature. It is in the row for New York, New York.

2. *Answer:* Fairbanks, Alaska

Explanation: Fairbanks shows a temperature of –13°F. This temperature is below or colder than 0°F.

3. *Answer/Explanation:* Alaska is much farther away from the equator than Florida, so it has a colder climate, and so its average January temperature would be colder than Florida's. **OR** Florida is much closer to the equator than Alaska, so it has a much warmer climate, and so the average January temperature would be much warmer than Alaska's.

Constructed Response Question 4

1. *Answer:* 54%

Explanation: Find the row labeled 1976 and read across to the second column labeled % of Eligible Voters Who Voted. The number in the row for 1976 is 54%.

2. *Answer:* 1992

Explanation: Look at the % of Eligible Voters Who Voted column. The numbers decrease or go down each election, until 1992, when it increased from 50% in 1988 to 55% in 1992.

3. *Answer/Explanation:* There are several correct answers to this question. They may include to participate in government, to pick people whom we think will be good leaders, to pick leaders whose ideas we like, to take advantage of the privilege of voting because we shouldn't waste it, to make our opinions count. If your answer isn't here, check with a grown-up to see if you answered the question correctly. Most reasonable answers will be accepted.

DOCUMENT-BASED SCAFFOLDING QUESTIONS

Document 1

1. The Wright Brothers made and flew the first successful airplane.

Document 2

1. *Answer/Explanation:* There are five possible answers to this question: electromagnetic telegraph, typewriter, telephone, phonograph, or wireless telegraph. You must have one of these answers for A and one for B.

Document 3

1. *Answer/Explanation:* 44,000 miles. To find this answer you would need to set up the following math problem:

$$
\begin{array}{r}
53{,}000 \\
-\ 9{,}000 \\
\hline
44{,}000 \text{ miles}
\end{array}
$$

Document 4

1. *Answer/Explanation:* Increase. The numbers in the % Living in Urban Areas column went up or increased every year shown on the chart.

Document 5

1. *Answer/Explanation:* Henry Ford was able to make his cars cheaper and faster because of the moving assembly line.

Sample Essay

The communities in America changed a lot during the 1800s and early 1900s. Most of this change happened because of changes in technology. Improvements in transportation, communication, and manufacturing made life in America different forever.

One way that communities changed was the way in which they communicated with each other. One example of this is the invention of the electromagnetic telegraph in 1837. This allowed people to send messages to each other without writing letters and waiting for them to arrive. Another improvement in communication came with the invention of the telephone in 1876. This allowed people to communicate instantly with each other, even if the other person was in another town!

A second way that communities changed involved transportation. Several inventions allowed people and goods to travel to places that they would not have been able to before. For example, the Wright brothers dreamed of being able to fly like the birds. Today many of us have flown somewhere; it is much faster than driving. Another change in transportation was the railroads. By 1870 there were over 53,000 miles of railroad track all the way from the Atlantic Ocean to the Pacific Ocean. People were able to see parts of the country that they never could have seen before trains. Businesses were also able to ship goods quickly and cheaply all over the country. Perhaps the biggest change in people's everyday lives came with the cheap cars called Model T Fords. Henry Ford was able to sell them in 1926 for only $290. He was able to make them and sell them so cheaply because of an improvement in manufacturing called the moving assembly line. It moved the car from person to person as the car was being built to save time. Many people bought these cars, and their lives were changed. Today, almost everyone I know has a car. They changed our communities forever.

A third way that technology changed our communities is by the types of communities that we live in. In 1830, about 91 percent of all Americans lived in rural or farming areas. Then transportation changed, communication changed, and manufacturing changed. Because of all of these changes, we needed more people to work in factories and offices than on farms. So by 1950, almost 60 percent of Americans lived in urban or city-type areas. This is probably the biggest change in our communities.

As you can see, life has changed forever. We are not the same country that we were 200 years ago. Technology is constantly changing our lives. I sometimes wonder what the world will be like 200 years in the future . . . I am sure it will be very, very different!

This essay would earn a score of 4 out of 4. It is well organized, detailed, and clear. A very important part of earning such a good score is to include information from each of the documents. This essay does that; it even uses some of the answers to the scaffolding questions right in the essay.

Appendix A

Vocabulary

A.D. Used to label dates that occurred after the year 0. For example, the Declaration of Independence was signed in the year 1776 A.D.

Algonkian A group of Native American Tribes that shared a common language and settled in the southeastern part of New York State.

Articles of Confederation (1781–1789) The first Constitution of the Untied States. It gave little power to the central government and a lot of power to individual states. This proved to be a problem, and the current Constitution was adopted.

Artifact Something made by humans. We often study artifacts to learn about other cultures.

Battle of Saratoga (1777) Revolutionary War battle that is considered by many to be the turning point of the war. Fought near Saratoga, New York. American colonists won the battle. The victory helped to convince France to support the colonists against England.

Battle of Yorktown (1781) Last major battle of the Revolutionary War. Colonists won the battle.

Battles of Lexington and Concord (1775) The first battles of the Revolutionary War.

B.C. Used to label dates that occurred before the year 0. For example, we believe that Native Americans came to this continent in about 20,000 B.C.

Bill of Rights Amendments 1–10 of the United States Constitution. These amendments guarantee individual liberties to Americans. For example, the First Amendment guarantees freedom of religion and freedom of speech.

Boundary Line A line on a map marking the end of one area and the beginning of another. For example, a national boundary shows the end of the United States and the beginning of Canada. A state boundary line shows where New York ends and Pennsylvania begins.

Budget A plan to organize how we spend or save the money that we earn.

Capital City The city that is the center of government for a state or country. For example, Albany is the capital of New York State. Washington, D.C. is the capital of the United States.

Cardinal Directions The four main directions found on a compass or compass rose: north, south, east, and west.

Cartier, Jacques The French explorer who explored and discovered the St. Lawrence River area.

Century 100 years.

Champlain, Samuel de French explorer who explored and set up Quebec and explored the Lake Champlain area.

Checks and Balances The way in which the three branches of our government check each other to make sure that one branch does not take too much power. For example, the president can veto (not approve) a law that Congress has passed. Another example is that the Supreme Court has the power to declare a law that Congress has made unconstitutional.

Chronological Order The order that things happened.

Citizenship The rights and responsibilities of being a citizen. For example, it is your right to vote when you are 18 years old. It is your responsibility to serve the country by being on jury duty in a trial.

Civilization The culture of a time period or region.

Colonial Period The time period during which part of the Americas were colonies of Great Britain before becoming independent and creating the United States.

Colony An area of land that is governed by another country, which may be far away.

Community A group of people who live in the same area and help each other to meet their needs and wants.

Conflict Resolution The way in which people solve disagreements.

Constitution of New York The written plan for the government of New York State.

Constitution of the United States of America The written plan for the government of the United States of America. It includes three parts.

Name of the Part	Purpose
Preamble	An introduction; states the purpose of the Constitution
Articles	The body; explains how the government will work, what each branch of government is responsible for, and who will be in each branch of government
Amendments	Those things that have been changed or added to the Constitution

Consumer A person who buys goods or services to meet their own needs and wants.

Continent One of the seven main land parts of the earth: Africa, Antarctica, Asia, Australia, Europe, North America, and South America.

Continental Congress (1775) Colonists who met in 1775 to decide what to do about their problems with England.

Culture The customs, traditions, and way of life of a group of people in a certain area or time period.

Custom Something that happens in a culture because it is expected or is a tradition. For example, it is an American custom to have fireworks on the Fourth of July.

Decade Ten years.

Declaration of Independence The document that the colonies sent to Great Britain saying that they wanted to be free from British rule. It was written mainly by Thomas Jefferson and adopted on July 4, 1776.

Democracy A government in which the people are part of making decisions, usually through voting.

Diverse Different.

Ellis Island An island in New York Harbor. Ellis Island was the country's main immigration station from 1892 to 1924. Today there is an immigration museum on the island.

Environment The things that are in your surroundings.

Equality When things are equal for all.

Equator The imaginary line that is 0 degrees latitude. It runs around the earth halfway between the North and South Poles. It divides the earth into Northern and Southern Hemispheres.

Era A time period.

Erie Canal The canal that connects Buffalo and Albany. It was opened in 1825. It made transporting goods cheaper and faster.

European Someone or something from Europe, including Great Britain, France, Spain, Italy, Holland, and Germany.

Expenses The things that you must pay for, such as gas, a home, and a car.

Explorer A person who explores and investigates a new place to find out more about it.

Export Something that a community sells to another community. For example, Brazil exports cashew and Brazil nuts to North America.

Fact/Opinion A fact is something that is true or has really happened. An opinion is something that is your understanding or viewpoint about something. For example,

Fact: Buffalo is a city in New York State.
Opinion: Samantha is the nicest person in Buffalo.

French and Indian War War between Britain and France and their Native American Allies. The war was fought over land claims. Britain won the war. The war was fought between 1754 and 1759. It ended with a treaty in 1763.

Geography The study of the earth's surface.

Globe A model of the earth that is the same shape as the earth, a sphere.

Goods Things that meet people's needs and wants, such as lumber and clothing.

Government The people whose job it is to set goals for a place, make laws, and keep a place running smoothly to make people safe and happy.

Hemisphere Half of a sphere, usually used to refer to half of the earth. For example, the Eastern Hemisphere or the Southern Hemisphere.

Hodenosaunee Means "the people of the longhouse." This is the proper name to refer to those tribes that are commonly known as the Iroquois. See *Iroquois Confederacy*.

Hudson, Henry English explorer who explored the Hudson River for the Dutch.

Immigration The act of coming to a new country with the purpose of living there.

Import Something that a community buys from another community. For example, the United States imports oil from other countries.

Income The money that you earn from your job.

Industrialization When an area becomes a region of machines, factories, and many homes. Usually going from an agricultural region to one with many factories.

Interdependence The way in which people and places depend on each other to help meet their needs and wants.

Intermediate Directions Those directions found on a compass or compass rose, between the cardinal directions: northeast, southeast, southwest, northwest.

Iroquois Confederacy The name given to the tribes of central and western New York that joined together to provide for a common defense against enemies. These tribes include the Seneca, Mohawk, Onondaga, Oneida, Cayuga, and later, the Tuscarora. See also *Hodenosaunee*.

Justice Fairness.

Latitude The distance north or south of the equator, measured in degrees. Lines of latitude are imaginary lines that run parallel to the equator and are sometimes called parallels.

Laws Rules that a whole community agrees to.

Liberty Freedom.

Lobsterbacks A nickname given to the British soldiers during the Revolutionary War because of their red coats.

Longhouse The traditional shelter used by the Iroquois/Hodenosaunee. It could be as long as 300 feet and as wide as 20 feet and housed many families.

Longitude The distance east or west of the prime meridian, measured in degrees. Lines of longitude are lines that run north and south connecting the North and South Poles. They are sometimes called *meridians*.

Loyalist A colonist who stayed loyal to the British during the Revolutionary War.

Map A flat picture of the earth or part of the earth. There are several kinds of maps.

Type of Map	Purpose
Political	Shows the boundaries and borders of places, and labels cities and countries
Physical	Shows naturally occurring things such as mountains and rivers
Historical	Shows where events of the past happened
Transportation	Shows routes to travel from one place to another

Mayflower Compact (1620) The document signed by male passengers of the *Mayflower* before landing at Plymouth. It served as the foundation for their government.

Migration When people or animals move from one place to another.

Militia An army made of citizens, not soldiers. The colonists formed a militia to fight against the British.

Millennium 1,000 years.

National Holidays

Name of the National Holiday	Month Celebrated	Purpose
New Year's Day	January	To celebrate the first day of the year
Martin Luther King, Jr. Day	January	To honor Dr. King, a leader of the civil rights movement
President's Day	February	To honor our presidents—originally to celebrate Washington's and Lincoln's birthdays
Memorial Day	May	To honor those that have died in service to our country
Independence Day	July	To celebrate the signing of the Declaration of Independence
Labor Day	September	To honor working people and all that they do for our country
Columbus Day	October	To honor the explorer Columbus
Veteran's Day	November	To celebrate those people who have served in the military and to honor those people who have died in our wars
Thanksgiving Day	November	To give thanks—originally a harvest festival, which celebrated the harvesting of crops
Christmas Day	December	A religious holiday celebrated in some religions

Native American A member of any of the tribes of peoples thought to be the earliest inhabitants of the Americas. Mistakenly called Indians by Columbus because he thought he was in the Indies.

Needs and Wants Needs are those things that you must have for survival: food, shelter, water, clothing. Wants are those things that you don't need to have to survive but would like, usually to make your life better, such as books, jewelry, and music.

Neighborhood The area around your home.

New Netherland Founded in 1624 by the Dutch along the Hudson River. Captured by the British in 1664, when it was renamed New York.

New York Founded in 1664. The name that the British gave to the area that is today New York State. It is named after the Duke of York.

Patriot A colonist who wanted independence from the British during the Revolutionary War.

Patriotism The ways in which we show our love and respect for our country and its symbols.

Pledge of Allegiance The words that we say to promise our loyalty to our country.

Population The number of people living in an area.

Prime Meridian The imaginary line that is 0 degrees longitude. It runs north and south and connects the North and South Poles. It runs though Greenwich, England and is sometimes called the Greenwich Meridian. It divides the earth into the Eastern and Western Hemispheres.

Producer A person who makes things (goods) or provides services to help people to meet their needs and wants.

Redcoats A nickname given to the British soldiers during the Revolutionary War because of their red coats.

Resource Something that is found within an area and can be used to meet people's needs or wants. There are three main kinds of resources.

Type of Resource	Definition
Natural Resource	Something that occurs in nature such as trees, water, and coal
Capital Resource	Money
Human Resource	The people

Revolutionary War (1775–1783) The war fought between American colonists and British soldiers to gain the Americans' independence from Britain. The American colonists won the war.

Rules Behaviors that people agree to in order to keep things orderly and safe.

Rural An area described as the country, which often has many farms.

Savings The money that you put aside to use later.

Scale of Miles The scale on a map that is used to show what a distance on a map is equal to in real life. For example, 1 inch = 5 miles.

Scarcity When the demand for something is greater than the supply.

Services Actions that are performed by people such as doctors, builders, and hairdressers to help other people meet their needs and wants.

Slave A person who has been bought by another person for the purpose of work without pay.

Suburban An area of land that is connected to a city, consisting mainly of homes and shops.

Taxes Money paid to the government, which is used to provide services and facilities for the public.

Three Branches of Government The constitution of the United States divides the government into three branches: legislative, executive, and judicial.

Branch	Members	Examples of Powers
Legislative	Congress: House of Representatives and the Senate	To tax To declare war To make laws
Executive	President	Commander in Chief of Armed Forces To make agreements with other countries
Judicial	Courts: Head court is the Supreme Court	To interpret the constitution

Timeline A visual way to represent events in chronological order.

Traditions Customs that are handed down in families.

Transportation The way in which people and goods are moved from one place to another. For example, forms of transportation include wagons, horses, trains, cars, airplanes, and boats.

Urban An area of land usually described as a city.

Urbanization The process by which an area changes from rural to urban.

Verrazzano, Giovanni da Italian explorer who explored for France. He was the first European explorer to discover the land that is now called New York State, exploring the New York Bay area.

Appendix B

New York State Curriculum Outline for Grade 3

A Note for Teachers, Parents, and Students:

This is the content for the New York State Social Studies Curriculum Grade 3. This tells you what facts you should remember from third grade.

GRADE 3: COMMUNITIES AROUND THE WORLD—LEARNING ABOUT PEOPLE AND PLACES

In the Grade 3 social studies program, students study about communities throughout the world. The five social studies standards form the basis for this investigation as students learn about the social, political, geographic, economic, and historic characteristics of different world communities. Students learn about communities that reflect the diversity of the world's peoples and cultures. They study Western and non-Western examples from a variety of geographic areas. Students also begin to learn about historic chronology by placing important events on timelines. Students locate world communities and learn how different communities meet their basic needs and wants. Students begin to compare the roles of citizenship and the kinds of governments found in various world communities.

Cultures and Civilizations

- What is a culture? What is a civilization?
- How and why do cultures change?
- Where do people settle and live? Why?
- People in world communities exchange elements of their cultures.
- People in world communities use legends, folktales, oral histories, biographies, autobiographies, and historical narratives to transmit values, ideas, beliefs, and traditions.
- People in world communities celebrate their accomplishments, achievements, and contributions.
- Historic events can be viewed through the eyes of those who were there, as shown in their art, writings, music, and artifacts.

Communities Around the World

- People of similar and different cultural groups often live together in world communities.
- World communities have social, political, economic, and cultural similarities and differences.
- World communities change over time.
- Important events and eras of the near and distant past can be displayed on timelines.
- Calendar time can be measured in terms of years, decades, centuries, and millennia, using B.C. and A.D. as reference points.
- All people in world communities need to learn, and they learn in different ways.
- Families in world communities differ from place to place.
- Beliefs, customs, and traditions in world communities are learned from others and may differ from place to place.

- Different events, people, problems, and ideas make up world communities.
- People in world communities may have different interpretations and perspectives about important issues and historic events.

The Location of World Communities

- World communities can be located on maps and globes (latitude and longitude).
- The spatial relationships of world communities can be described by direction, location, distance, and scale.
- Regions represent areas of Earth's surface with unifying geographic characteristics.
- World communities can be located in relation to each other and to principal parallels and meridians.
- Geographic representations such as aerial photographs and satellite-produced images can be used to locate world communities.
- Earth's continents and oceans can be located in relation to each other and to principal parallels and meridians.

Physical, Human, and Cultural Characteristics of World Communities

- The causes and effects of human migration vary in different world regions.
- The physical, human, and cultural characteristics of different regions and people throughout the world are different.
- Interactions between economic activities and geographic factors differ in world communities.
- The factors that influence human settlements differ in world communities.

People Depending On and Modifying Their Physical Environments

- People living in world communities depend on and modify their physical environments in different ways.
- Lifestyles in world communities are influenced by environmental and geographic factors.
- The development of world communities is influenced by environmental and geographic factors.

Challenge of Meeting Needs and Wants in World Communities

- Societies organize their economies to answer three fundamental economic questions: What goods and services should be produced and in what quantities? How shall goods and services be produced? For whom shall goods and services be produced?
- Human needs and wants differ from place to place.
- People in world communities make choices due to unlimited needs and wants and limited resources.
- People in world communities must depend on others to meet their needs and wants.
- Production, distribution, exchange, and consumption of goods and services are economic decisions all societies must make.
- People in world communities use human, capital, and natural resources.
- People in world communities locate, develop, and make use of natural resources.
- Resources are important to economic growth in world communities.

Economic Decision Making in World Communities

- Production, distribution, exchange, and consumption of goods and services are economic decisions that all world communities must make.
- Economic decisions in world communities are influenced by many factors.

Symbols of Citizenship in World Communities

- People in world communities celebrate various holidays and festivals.
- People in world communities use monuments and memorials to represent symbols of their nations.

People Making and Changing Rules and Laws

- People in world communities form governments to develop rules and laws to govern community members.
- People in world communities may have conflicts over rules, rights, and responsibilities.
- The processes of selecting leaders, solving problems, and making decisions differ in world communities.

Governments Around the World

- Governments in world communities organize to provide functions people cannot provide as individuals.
- Governments in world communities have the authority to make, carry out, and enforce laws and manage disputes among them.
- Governments in world communities develop rules and laws.
- Governments in world communities plan, organize, and make decisions.

Appendix C

New York State Curriculum Outline for Grade 4

A Note for Teachers, Parents, and Students:

This is the content for the New York State Social Studies Curriculum Grade 4. This tells you what facts you should remember from fourth grade.

GRADE 4: LOCAL HISTORY AND LOCAL GOVERNMENT

The Grade 4 social studies program builds on the students' understanding of families, schools, and communities and highlights the political institutions and historic development of their local communities with connections to New York State and the United States. The in-depth study of local government will emphasize the structure and function of the different branches and the roles of civic leaders. Students continue to learn about the rights, responsibilities, and duties of citizenship. By participating in school activities that teach democratic values, students develop a sense of political efficacy and a better understanding of the roles of supporters and leaders. Students expand their civic concepts of power, equality, justice, and citizenship as they learn about local government.

The historic study of local communities focuses on the social/cultural, political, and economic factors that helped to shape these communities. Students study about the significant people, places, events, and issues that influenced life in their local communities. Students can investigate local events and issues and connect them to national events and issues. The Grade 4 program should consider the following themes and events at the local level: Native American Indians of New York State, the European encounter, the colonial and Revolutionary War period, the new nation, and the period of industrial growth and development in New York State. This chronological framework will help students to organize information about local history and connect it to United States history.

Connect Local, New York State, and United States History, Focusing on the Following Themes

- Native American Indians of New York State
- European encounter: three worlds (Europe, Africa, and the Americas) meet in the Americas
- Colonial and Revolutionary periods
- The new nation
- Industrial growth and expansion
- Government—local and state

Native American Indians of New York State

- The first inhabitants of our local region and state—Native American Indians
- Early inhabitants of our state—the Iroquois (Haudenosaunee—people of the longhouse) and the Algonquian
- Meeting basic needs—food, clothing, and shelter
- Uses of the environment and how Native American Indian settlements were influenced by environmental and geographic factors
- Important accomplishments and contributions of Native American Indians who lived in our community and state

Three Worlds (Europe, the Americas, Africa) Meet in the Americas

- Major explorers of New York State
- Impacts of exploration—social/cultural, economic, political, and geographic
- The slave trade and slavery in the colonies
- Groups of people who migrated to our local region and into our state
- Ways that people depended on and modified their physical environments

Colonial and Revolutionary Periods

- Dutch, English, and French influences in New York State
- Lifestyles in the colonies—comparisons during different time periods
- Different types of daily activities including social/cultural, political, economic, scientific/technological, or religious
- Ways that colonists depended on and modified their physical environments
- Cultural similarities and differences, including folklore, ideas, and other cultural contributions that helped shape our community, local region, and state
- Colonial governments
- Colonial societies were organized to answer three fundamental economic questions: What goods and services do we produce? How do we produce them? For whom do we produce them?
- Ways of making a living in our local region and state
- Causes for revolution: social, political, economic
- Important accomplishments of individuals and groups living in our community and region

The Revolutionary War in New York State

- Location of New York State
- The significance of New York State's location and its relationship to the locations of other people and places
- Geographic features that influenced the war
- Native American Indians in New York State influenced the war
- The war strategy: Saratoga and other local battles
- Loyalists and patriots in New York State
- Leaders of the Revolution
- Effects of the Revolutionary War

The New Nation

- Foundations for a new government and the ideals of American democracy as expressed in the Mayflower Compact, the Declaration of Independence, and the Constitutions of the State of New York and the United States of America
- The importance of the Bill of Rights
- Individuals and groups who helped to strengthen democracy in the United States
- The roots of American culture, how it developed from many different traditions, and the ways many people from a variety of groups and backgrounds played a role in creating it
- Those values, practices, and traditions that unite all Americans

Industrial Growth and Expansion

- Transportation, inventions, communication, and technology (e.g., 1800s—Erie Canal, railroads, steamboats, turnpikes, telegraph, cable; 1900s—automobiles, subways, air travel, seaways, telephones, radios and televisions, computer)

- Immigration and migration (e.g., Ellis Island; the mass starvation in Ireland, 1845–1850; forced relocation of Native American Indians in New York State)
- The important contributions of immigrants to New York State
- Geographic influences of industrialization and expansion (e.g., natural resources, location); the interactions between economic and geographic factors

Urbanization: Economic, Political, and Social Impacts

- Rural to urban to suburban migration
- Economic interdependence (e.g., resource use; from farm to market)
- Ways of learning and public education in our community and state
- The labor movement and child labor

Government

- Basic democratic values (taken from *National Standards for Civics and Government*)
- The fundamental values of American democracy include an understanding of the following concepts: individual rights to life, liberty, property, and the pursuit of happiness; the public or common good; justice; equality of opportunity; diversity; truth; and patriotism.
- The fundamental values and principles of American democracy are expressed in the Declaration of Independence, Preamble to the United States Constitution, Bill of Rights, Pledge of Allegiance, speeches, songs, and stories.

Purposes of Government

- The basic purposes of government in the United States are to protect the rights of individuals and to promote the common good (taken from *National Standards for Civics and Government*)

Local and State Governments

- An introduction to the probable consequences of the absence of government
- The structure and function of the branches of government of New York State and local governments, including executive, legislative, and judicial branches
- The meaning of key terms and concepts related to government, including democracy, power, and citizenship
- Development of the United States Constitution and the Constitution of the State of New York and their respective Bills of Rights as written plans for organizing the functions of government and safeguarding individual liberties
- Representatives in the legislative, executive, and judicial branches at the local, state, and national levels of government and how they are elected or appointed to office
- The election and/or appointment of leaders who make, enforce, and interpret laws
- Citizenship and the rules and responsibilities of citizenship in the classroom, school, home, and local community
- Citizenship includes an awareness of the holidays, celebrations, and symbols of our nation, including the flag of the United States of America, its proper display, and use
- Duties of effective, informed citizenship including voting, jury service, and other service to the local community
- Citizen participation in political decision making and problem solving at the local, state, and national levels

Appendix D

New York State Key Concepts for the K-12 Social Studies Program

A Note to Teachers and Parents:

These are the Key Concepts to be developed in the New York State Social Studies Curriculum Grades K–12. They are a part of the New York State Education Department Core Curriculum. To access any future changes or updates to these Key Concepts please visit: www.emsc.nysed.gov/ciai/cores.htm.

A Note to Students:

The Key Concepts of the New York State Social Studies Curriculum are the "big ideas" that we discussed in Chapter 6. These ideas are not something you can memorize or write a definition for in one sentence. They are the ideas that you will build and add to throughout your whole life.

You will probably know some of the words now, but you might learn some of them as you move on to the Middle and High Schools. If you do not understand some of the words, talk about it with a grown-up; he or she can help you to decide whether it is something you should learn more about before the test.

HISTORY:

Belief Systems: An established orderly way that groups of individuals look at religious faith or philosophical tenets.

Change: The basic alterations in things, events, and ideas.

Choice: The right or power to select from a range of alternatives.

Conflict: A clash of ideas, interests, or wills that results from incompatible opposing forces.

Culture: The patterns of human behavior that include ideas, beliefs, values, artifacts, and ways of making a living that any society transmits to succeeding generations to meet its fundamental needs.

Diversity: Understanding and respecting others and oneself including similarities and differences in language, gender, socioeconomic class, religion, and other human characteristics and traits.

Empathy: The ability to understand others through being able to identify in oneself responses similar to the experiences, behaviors, and responses of others.

Identity: Awareness of one's own values, attitudes, and capabilities as an individual and as a member of different groups.

Imperialism: The domination by one country of the political and/or economic life of another country or region.

Interdependence: Reliance upon others in mutually beneficial interactions and exchanges.

Movement of People and Goods: The constant exchange of people, ideas, products, technologies, and institutions from one region or civilization to another that has existed throughout history.

Nationalism: The feeling of pride in and devotion to one's country or the desire of a people to control their own government free from foreign interference or rule.

Urbanization: Movement of people from rural to urban areas.

GEOGRAPHY:

Environment and Society: The physical environment is modified by human activities, largely as a consequence of the ways in which human societies value and use earth's natural resources; human activities are also influenced by earth's physical features and processes.

Human Systems: People are central to geography in that human activities help shape earth's surface, human settlements and structures are part of earth's surface, and humans compete for control of earth's surface.

Physical Systems: Physical processes shape earth's surface and interact with plant and animal life to create, sustain, and modify ecosystems.

Places and Regions: The identities and lives of individuals and peoples are rooted in particular places and in those human constructs called *regions*.

The World in Spatial Terms: Geography studies the relationships between people, places, and environments by mapping information about them into a spatial context.

ECONOMICS:

Economic Systems: Traditional, command, market, and mixed systems. Each system must answer the three basic economic questions: What goods and services shall be produced and in what quantities? How shall these goods and services be produced? For whom shall goods and services be produced?

Factors of Production: Human, natural, and capital resources that when combined become various goods and services.

Needs and Wants: Those goods and services that are essential such as food, clothing, and shelter (needs), and those goods and services that people would like to have to improve the quality of their lives, (i.e., wants—education, security, health care, entertainment).

Scarcity: The conflict between unlimited needs and wants and limited natural and human resources.

Science and Technology: The tools and methods used by people to get what they need and want.

CIVICS, CITIZENSHIP, AND GOVERNMENT:

Citizenship: Membership in a community with its accompanying rights, responsibilities, and dispositions.

Civic Values: Those important principles that serve as the foundation for our democratic form of government. These values include justice, honesty, self-discipline, due process, equality, majority rule with respect for minority rights, and respect for self, others, and property.

Decision Making: The processes used to "monitor and influence public and civic life by working with others, clearly articulating ideals and interests, building coalitions, seeking consensus, negotiating compromise, and managing conflict."

Taken from: Civics Framework for the 1998 National Assessment of Educational Progress, NAEP Civics Consensus Project, The National Assessment Governing Board, United States Department of Education, p. 18

Government: "Formal institutions and processes of a politically organized society with authority to make, enforce, and interpret laws and other binding rules about matters of common interest and concern. Government also refers to the group of people, acting in formal political institutions at national, state, and local levels, who exercise decision-making power or enforce laws and regulations."

Taken from: Civics Framework, p. 19

Human Rights: Those basic political, economic, and social rights that all human beings are entitled to, such as the right to life, liberty, and the security of person, and a standard of living adequate for health and well-being of oneself and of one's family. Human rights are inalienable and expressed by various United Nations documents, including the United Nations Charter and the Universal Declaration of Human Rights.

Justice: The fair, equal, proportional, or appropriate treatment rendered to individuals in interpersonal, societal, or government interactions.

Nation–State: A geographic/political organization uniting people by a common government.

Political Systems: Monarchies, dictatorships, and democracies address certain basic questions of government such as: What should a government have the power to do? What should a government not have the power to do? A political system also provides for ways that parts of that system interrelate and combine to perform specific functions of government.

Powers: The ability of people to compel or influence the actions of others. "Legitimate power is called authority."

Appendix E

New York State Social Studies Skills for the K-12 Social Studies Program

A Note to Teachers and Parents:

These are the Social Studies Skills to be developed in the New York State Social Studies Curriculum Grades K–12. They are a part of the New York State Education Department Social Studies Program Overview. The focus of the skills is to ensure that you know how to gather and make meaning from the facts and that you know how to apply those facts to make decisions and solve problems. For further information regarding these skills, please visit: www.emsc.nysed.gov/ciai/socst/ssrg.html (look under "Overview").

A Note to Students:

The Skills of the New York State Social Studies Curriculum are not pieces of information you need to learn. Instead, the skills are what you do with the facts that you learn. For example, if you learn that colonial children in New York played checkers, went to school, and had chores, these are just facts. In order to make meaning out of those facts it is a good skill to be able to compare and contrast the life of a colonial child to your own life. Applying these skills to the facts makes them come alive and helps you to understand what it was truly like in colonial New York.

SOCIAL STUDIES SKILLS

GATHERING AND ANALYZING INFORMATION

Getting Information:

- Identify a variety of sources of information such as tables, graphs, charts, observations, field trips, maps, globes, newspapers, magazines, and so on.
- Recognize the advantages and disadvantages of those sources of information.
- Locate sources of print and nonprint information.
- Sort information to recognize the types and kinds that are relevant.
- Find information within the print and nonprint sources.
- Organize the information collected into notes, being sure to cite sources.

Using Information:

- Sort and classify data: ordering chronologically, placing in a table, graphing, mapping, and so on.
- Identify similarities and differences in data.
- Evaluate data by considering author's point of view, distinguishing facts from opinions, and so on.
- Draw inferences from data.
- Check on the completeness of data.
- Make generalizations from data.
- Think about other outcomes if different decisions had been made.

Presenting Information:

- Speak in an effective way.
- Engage in discussions as a leader or participant.
- Use media and visuals to communicate ideas.

- Write in an expository form using proper format of an introduction, body, and conclusion. Support generalizations through factual examples.
- Recognize, understand, and use nonverbal types of communication that exist in our culture and in others.

Participating in Interpersonal and Group Relations:

- Recognize that people have different points of view.
- Listen to reason.
- Observe others.
- Recognize and avoid stereotypes.
- Withhold judgments until all of the facts are known.
- Participate in group planning and discussions following democratic procedures to help the group make decisions.
- Assume responsibility for tasks when working alone or in a group.

PROBLEM-FINDING AND PROBLEM-SOLVING SKILLS

Finding Problems:

- Raise questions about problems. Not just who, what, when, and where; instead ask how and why.
- Use higher-level thinking skills to analyze a problem by considering the facts, concepts, vocabulary, and points of view.

Solve Problems That Are Presented by the Teacher or Identified by the Students Themselves:

- Write about a problem, clearly identifying the problem.
- Write a series of questions about the problem.
- Develop a plan to solve the problem.
- Obtain information related to the problem from a variety of sources.

- Evaluate the sources of information.
- Organize data related to the problem.
- When necessary redefine the problem in light of new information.
- Develop a product that summarizes the information learned, which should be shared orally, in writing, by demonstration, diagram, map, chart, and so on.

Work with Others Engaged in Problem-Finding/ Solving Skills:

- Participate in group planning and discussion.
- Incorporate a set of positive learning attitudes such as recognizing other points of view and listening to others.

Communicate Orally, Visually, and/or in Writing the Results of the Problem-Finding/Solving Efforts:

- Speak in an effective, well-prepared way.
- Use media and various visuals to communicate ideas.
- Use different forms of written expression and their proper forms.

Appendix F

Internet Resources for Students, Parents, and Teachers

Note to Teachers and Parents:

The Internet is a wonderful resource filled with a vast amount of information, some accurate and some not. In order to help you to navigate these resources, I recommend the following resources for their accuracy and content appropriateness. However, due to the ever-changing nature of the Internet, you should preview the content before using it with your child or students.

A Note to Students:

You should have learned everything that you need to know for the New York State Social Studies Test. But sometimes as you practice, you may notice that you need to refresh your memory about a topic. There are a lot of Web sites on the Internet and it is a difficult job to decide which ones might be helpful. Sadly, some of them contain incorrect information and you will want to avoid those. On the next few pages, you will find a list of reliable Web sites that want to help you to learn. You certainly don't need to look at all of them, but this list might be helpful for refreshing your memory. Before you go on the Internet, you should be sure that you have permission from an adult.

Economic Education Web (EcEdWeb) This Web site is a valuable source for students, parents, and teachers. You will find information about economic concepts as well as excellent lesson plans related to economics. *ecedweb.unomaha.edu/home.cfm*

Federal Resources for Educational Excellence: Teaching and Learning Resources from Federal Agencies This Web site provides links to all of the resources that have been created by federal government agencies that might contain useful information for student researchers in grades K–12. Extremely well organized and incredibly helpful! *www.free.ed.gov/index.cfm*

Kids.gov: The Official Kids Portal for the U.S. Government This Web site is designed for kids and educators. It gives age-appropriate information and links to sites related to government Web sites. *www.kids.gov*

The Library of Congress This Web site is a vast storehouse of information relating to our nation's past and present, including American Memory, which contains historical documents and resources. *www.loc.gov/index.html*

The Library of Congress: Country Studies This Web site is especially for researchers gathering information on countries around the world. It is up to date and very useful. *lcweb2.loc.gov/frd/cs/cshome.html*

The National Archives This Web site maintains the collections of important historical documents and photographs and is a valuable resource for students, teachers, and families searching for information. *www.archives.gov/*

The National Council on Economic Education This fantastic Web site is the official site of the National Council on Economic Education, a professional organization devoted to improving education in economics. This site is very useful for teachers, parents, and students. It gives information about economic concepts, lesson plans, and simulations and activities for students. Teachers may join this organization or simply keep updated by visiting the Web site.
www.ncee.net

The National Council for Geographic Education This Web site is the official site of the National Council for Geographic Education, a professional organization devoted to improving education in geography. Teachers may join this organization or simply keep updated by visiting the Web site.
www.ncge.org

The National Council for History Education This Web site is the official site of the National Council for History Education, a professional organization devoted to improving education in history. Teachers may join this organization or simply keep updated by visiting the Web site.
www.nche.net

National Geographic This Web site is an invaluable tool for learning about the people, places, and cultures of our world. It is filled with images, maps, and updated information. There is an excellent resource section just for teachers and one just for kids!
www.nationalgeographic.com/

New York State Archives This Web site is dedicated to the preservation of and sharing of documents related to the history of New York State. It offers many resources for teachers, students, and parents.
www.archives.nysed.gov/aindex.shtml

The New York State Council for the Social Studies This Web site is the official site for the professional organization of Social Studies in New York State. It provides information and links that are useful especially to teachers.
www.nyscss.org/index.cfm

U.S. Department of State for Youth This Web site is designed for young people; it is a part of the U.S. Department of State Web site. The site gives excellent information about this branch of the government, U.S. foreign relations, and excellent links to other Social Studies-related sites. This Web site also includes a special section for parents and teachers with lesson plans.
future.state.gov

University of the State of New York: State Education Department This Web site is the official site for education in New York State. It provides information for teachers, parents, and students. The information ranges from certification policies to curriculum and assessment information. In all curriculum areas, this site provides the most up-to-date information. It is highly recommended that all teachers visit this Web site often to stay informed of any curriculum changes or updates.
www.nysed.gov/

Appendix G

More Practice Questions: Multiple-Choice, Constructed Response, and Document-Based Questions

A Note to Students:

If you worked your way through this book, you have learned about the test, and practiced answering a lot of questions. Great job! This appendix contains more questions to apply all you have learned.

PRACTICE SET: MULTIPLE-CHOICE QUESTIONS AND ANSWERS

Directions: Please use your knowledge of social studies to choose the best answer to each of the following questions.

Sample A

The name of the island that is famous for welcoming many foreign immigrants to New York State and the United States is

A. Ellis Island.
B. Angel Island.
C. Cayuga Island.
D. Syracuse Island.

Sample B

Which type of map would be the best to use if you wanted to find out where the land with the highest elevation in New York State is?

A. a political map
B. a historical map
C. a road map
D. a physical or relief map

Sample C

The geographer's tool that is the most accurate model of the earth is

A. a historical map.
B. a compass rose.
C. a political map.
D. a globe.

Sample D

The imaginary line that runs halfway between the North and South Poles around the earth is called

A. intermediate directions.
B. the prime meridian.
C. the equator.
D. the legend.

Sample E

When the United States declared that they were no longer under British rule, the document that they issued was called what?

A. The Declaration of Independence
B. The Articles of Confederation
C. The Constitution
D. The Magna Carta

Sample F

The first 10 amendments to the Constitution are called the

A. Preamble.
B. Great Compromise.
C. Bill of Rights.
D. Article I.

Sample G

Millions of immigrants came to America to

A. seek their fortune.
B. escape religious and political persecution.
C. be granted individual freedoms.
D. All of the above.

Sample H

The money that people pay to their government in order to pay for services and things for their community is called

A. taxes.
B. interest.
C. voting.
D. salary.

Sample I

Profile of the 2000 U.S. Population by Age Group

Data Source: U.S. Census Bureau

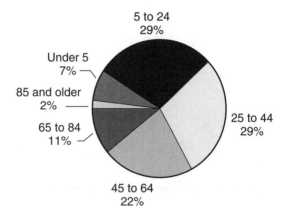

Which age group made up the smallest percentage of the U.S. population in 2000?

A. under 5 years old
B. 25–44 years old
C. 85+ years old
D. 65–84 years old

Sample J

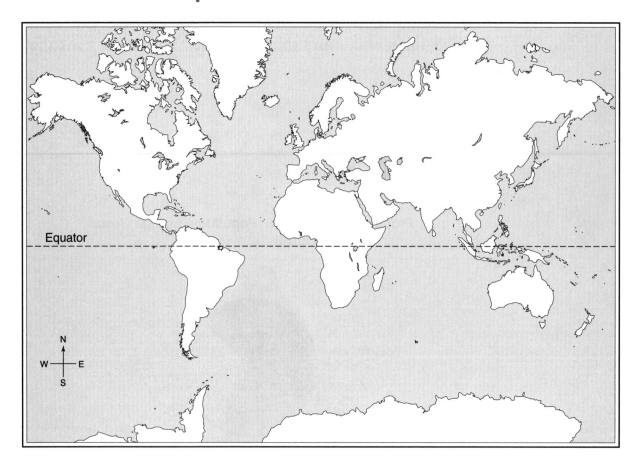

Which hemisphere contains the most land?

A. Northern Hemisphere
B. Southern Hemisphere
C. They are both equal.

ANSWERS AND EXPLANATIONS

A. *Answer:* (A) Ellis Island

Explanation: You can eliminate Choice C Cayuga Island and Choice D Syracuse Island because they are not islands. That leaves Choices A and B as our reasonable choices. Angel Island is an island that was used to process immigrants; however, it is on the west coast of our country. Ellis Island is the island found in New York Harbor and was used to process immigrants from all over the world as they came to America.

B. *Answer:* (D) a physical or relief map

Explanation: In this question, all the answers are reasonable because they are all kinds of maps. So you need to think about the purpose of each map so that you can eliminate it. A political map shows boundaries, cities, and capitals. It would not tell the elevation or height above sea level of the land. So Choice A is not the correct answer. You can eliminate Choice B because historical maps tell about the land long ago and usually show important locations related to an important historical event. This would not help us to know the elevation of the land. Choice C is not the correct answer. A road map is made to show where there are roads. This type of map helps you to get from one place to another. Only a physical or relief map is made to show the elevation of the land; it usually does this by using different colors to show different elevations.

C. *Answer:* (D) a globe

Explanation: After carefully reading this question, you can eliminate Choice B because a compass rose is not a model of the earth. Although both a historical map and a political map are representations of the earth, they are not models of the earth. Therefore, neither Choice A or C is the correct answer. A globe is considered to be the most accurate representation of the earth because it is the same shape as the earth, a sphere.

D. *Answer:* (C) the equator

Explanation: Choices A and D can be eliminated because "intermediate directions" and "legend" are geography terms; they are not the names of any lines of latitude or longitude. The two choices that are left are the prime meridian and the equator. People often confuse these two terms so it is important to read the description carefully and to visualize what the description is explaining. The prime meridian connects the North Pole and South Pole; however, the question asks for the imaginary line that runs halfway between the two poles. This describes the equator. Choice B is not the correct answer.

E. *Answer:* (A) The Declaration of Independence

Explanation: This question asks you to recall a very important document in American history. The other three choices are all related to our government, but the one that is correct is the Declaration of Independence. This question is a good example of how common sense can help you to figure out answers that you are not sure of. In this question, you are asked which document declared that the colonists were no longer under British rule. Think this through; a document that declares something is called a declaration. And if you are no longer under someone's rule, then you are independent. So the very question actually gives you the title of the document, The Declaration of Independence. So, even if you don't know the answer right away, try to reason your way through the question.

F. *Answer:* (C) Bill of Rights

Explanation: In this question, we can eliminate Choice B because the Great Compromise is not a part of the Constitution; it is the name for the agreement that was made when our founding fathers were trying to agree on how to govern our country and write the Constitution. The remaining three answers are actually all reasonable because they are all names of parts of our Constitution. We need to remember the purpose of each part of the Constitution so that we can eliminate several choices. We can eliminate the Preamble, Choice A, because it is the statement that is used as an introduction to the Constitution. It explains why the Constitution was written. We can also eliminate Choice D, Article I, because the articles are the part of the Constitution that explains how the government is run. The correct answer is the Bill of Rights. These ten amendments were added to the Constitution to make sure that the government guaranteed certain rights and freedoms.

G. *Answer:* (D) all of the above

Explanation: This question is another good example of why reading all the choices is very important. As you read through the choices, you might be confused because they all seem right. When this happens, look to see if there is a choice that includes all of the answers, as there was in this question. It is the correct answer.

H. *Answer:* (A) taxes

Explanation: This question is trying to find out if you remember the vocabulary word *taxes*, as well as to check if you understand why we pay them. The definitions of the other words do not match what was asked; therefore, they are not the correct answer.

I. *Answer:* (C) 85+ years old

Explanation: This question asks you to use another skill, reading circle graphs. The best strategy is to carefully find each age group listed and record their population percentage. Then compare the data and choose the best answer.

J. *Answer:* (A) Northern Hemisphere

Explanation: This question asks you to use the skill of map reading. By examining the world map that you are given, you can see that most of the land is in the Northern Hemisphere.

PRACTICE SET: CONSTRUCTED RESPONSE QUESTIONS AND ANSWERS

When you try these constructed response questions, try to use the following steps:

- Read the directions carefully.
- Take your time and analyze the document carefully.
- Read each question carefully to be sure that you understand what is being asked.
- Remember the CRQ pattern that we talked about.
- Use your knowledge of social studies and the document to help you to answer the questions.

When you are finished, check the answers and explanations. Good luck!

SAMPLE QUESTIONS

Sample A

Directions: Please use your knowledge of social studies and the map to answer Questions 1–3.

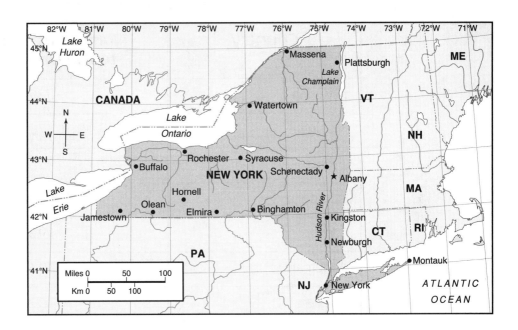

1. What is the name of the ocean that borders New York State?

   _____

   _____

2. Name two cities in New York State that can be found east of Rochester on this map.

   _____

   _____

3. Give the approximate latitude and longitude of Watertown, New York.

   _____

   _____

Sample B

Directions: Please use your knowledge of social studies and the chart to answer Questions 1–3.

A Sample of United States Immigration Statistics for 2006

Country	Number of Immigrants to the United States
Mexico	173,753
China	87,345
Peru	21,718
Jamaica	24,976
India	61,369
Vietnam	30,695
Japan	8,265
Canada	18,207
Philippines	74,607
Cuba	45,614

Data Source: US Department of Homeland Security

1. From which country shown on the chart did the most immigrants come in 2006?

_____

2. Did more immigrants come from Cuba or Vietnam in 2006?

_____

3. Does this chart give you more information about immigration from Europe or Asia in 2006?

_____

Sample C

Directions: Please use your knowledge of social studies and the charts to answer Questions 1–3.

A Sample of United States Imports and Exports in the Year 2007

Item	Exports*
Computers	13,506
Coffee	4
Nuts	3,448
Books	5,548
Diamonds	12,328
Toys/Games/ Sporting Goods	11,265

Item	Imports*
Computers	40,919
Coffee	1,275
Nuts	1,223
Books	4,638
Diamonds	18,952
Toys/Games/ Sporting Goods	34,362

Data Source: U.S. Census Bureau, Foreign Trade Division
Amounts are shown in millions of dollars.

1. Name one item, shown in the charts, that the United States exports.

   _____

   _____

2. Name one item that the United States exports more than it imports.

   _____

   _____

   _____

3. Give one reason why countries might import items.

   _____

   _____

   _____

Sample D

Directions: Please use your knowledge of social studies and this document to answer Questions 1–3.

The American's Creed

I believe in the United States of America as a government of the people, by the people, for the people; whose just powers are derived from the consent of the governed; a democracy in a republic; a sovereign Nation of many sovereign States; a perfect union, one and inseparable; established upon those principles of freedom, equality, justice and humanity for which American patriots sacrificed their lives and fortunes. I therefore believe it is my duty to my country to love it, to support its Constitution, to obey its laws, to respect its flag, and to defend it against all enemies.

—William Tyler Page, Clerk of the United States House of Representatives wrote The American's Creed in 1917. It was accepted by the House of Representatives on behalf of the American people on April 3, 1918.

1. Who is the author of *The American's Creed*?

   _____

2. According to *The American's Creed*, what is one of the principles, or ideas, that our government is established on?

   _____

3. According to this document, name one way that we can show our respect for our country.

   _____

Sample E

Directions: Please use your knowledge of social studies and the graph to answer Questions 1 and 2.

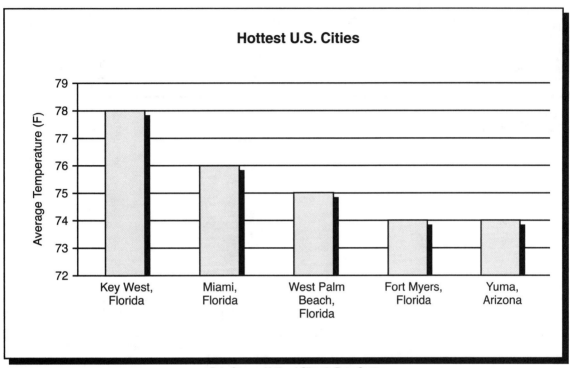

Data Source: National Climatic Data Center

1. What is the average yearly temperature in Yuma, Arizona?

   _____

   _____

2. How much warmer is the average daily temperature in Miami, Florida, than in West Palm Beach, Florida?

   _____

   _____

   _____

Sample F

Directions: Please use your knowledge of social studies and the timeline to answer Questions 1–3.

Timeline of the Erie Canal

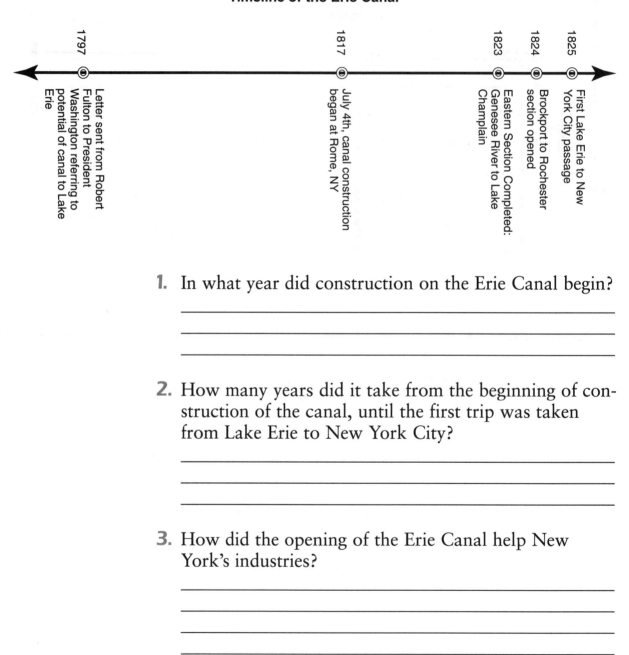

1. In what year did construction on the Erie Canal begin?

   _____

   _____

   _____

2. How many years did it take from the beginning of construction of the canal, until the first trip was taken from Lake Erie to New York City?

   _____

   _____

   _____

3. How did the opening of the Erie Canal help New York's industries?

   _____

   _____

   _____

   _____

Sample G

Directions: Please use your knowledge of social studies and this painting to answer Questions 1–3.

Signing the Declaration of Independence, 1776
Courtesy of Yale University Art Gallery

1. What year was the Declaration of Independence signed?

   _____

2. What country were the colonists declaring their independence from?

   _____

3. What war followed this declaration?

   _____

ANSWERS AND EXPLANATIONS

Sample A

1. *Answer:* The Atlantic Ocean

Explanation: Look at the map of New York carefully and find the Atlantic Ocean, shown bordering the southeast part of the state.

2. *Answer:* There are several possible answers for this question. You should have written two of the following choices: Elmira, Ithaca, Syracuse, Binghamton, Kingston, Newburgh, New York City, Montauk, Albany, Schenectady, Plattsburgh, Massena, Watertown.

Explanation: To answer this question, you must first locate the city of Rochester. Then using the Compass Rose to show you direction, find two cities that are east of Rochester.

3. *Answer:* About 76 W longitude and 44 N latitude

Explanation: This question is a typical third question; however, what you are being asked to remember from school is not a fact, but a skill. The question asks you to use the skill of finding latitude and longitude. To answer this question you must first find Watertown. Look at the grid lines shown on the map; these are the lines of latitude and longitude. The horizontal line that Watertown is closest to is labeled 44 N. This is the line of latitude. The vertical line that Watertown is closest to is labeled 76 W. This is the line of longitude.

Sample B

1. *Answer:* Mexico

Explanation: Look at the chart and find the largest number (173,753). This number belongs to Mexico.

2. *Answer:* Cuba

Explanation: You should find the number of immigrants who came from Cuba (45,614) and the number who came from Vietnam (30,695). Then compare these two numbers. 45,614 is the greater number; therefore, more immigrants came from Cuba than from Vietnam.

3. *Answer:* Asia

Explanation: To answer this question, you must remember learning about the different continents. If you look at the list, you will see that several countries are found in Asia, for example, China, Vietnam, and Japan, yet no countries listed in the chart are in Europe. Therefore, the graph shows more information about immigration from Asia than Europe in 2006.

Sample C

1. *Answer:* Any one of the following: computers, coffee, nuts, books, diamonds, toys, games, sporting goods

Explanation: The chart shows a sample of U.S. exports and imports; therefore, any item listed with a dollar amount in the export column is a product that the U.S. exports.

2. *Answer:* Either books or nuts

Explanation: Both books and nuts have a larger number in the exports column than they do in the imports column.

3. *Answer:* Reasonable and acceptable answers include: The country cannot produce the product themselves, or the country cannot produce enough of the product to fulfill the demand for it.

Explanation: In this question, the answer could be explained in many ways; therefore, variations are acceptable. However, it is important to note that the two reasons listed here are the main reasons that countries import items.

Sample D

1. *Answer:* William Tyler Page

Explanation: The author's name is written under the quotation.

2. *Answer:* One of the following: freedom, equality, justice, or humanity

Explanation: Even though this is the second question, it is a typical first question; the answer is found right in the document. The phrase found in the document begins "established upon those principles of" and then lists the principles of freedom, equality, justice, and humanity.

3. *Answer:* One of the following answers is acceptable: love our country, support the constitution, obey the laws, respect our flag, or defend against enemies. Other reasonable answers could also be accepted.

Explanation: This is an interesting question. You could have found the answer to the question right in the document, or you could have drawn from your own knowledge of ways that we can show respect for our country. An example would be by pledging allegiance to our flag. This is an acceptable answer that is not directly stated in the document.

Sample E

1. *Answer:* 74°F

Explanation: The bar for Yuma reaches to the line for 74.

2. *Answer:* 1°F

Explanation: The average temperature in Miami is 76°F and the average temperature in West Palm Beach is 75°F. To see how much warmer Miami is, you need to subtract 75°F from 76°F. The difference is 1°F.

Sample F

1. *Answer:* 1817

Explanation: Find the description which reads "July 4th, canal construction began at Rome, NY." This is shown at the marker for the year 1817.

2. *Answer:* 8 years

Explanation: In the first question, we found that construction of the canal began in 1817. To answer this question, we must find that the first trip from Lake Erie to New York City was taken in 1825. To find how many years it took from the beginning of construction until this trip, we must subtract. You should subtract the year construction began from the year this trip was taken. Set up your problem like this:

$$\begin{array}{r} 1825 \\ -1817 \\ \hline 8 \text{ years} \end{array}$$

3. *Answer:* There are several acceptable answers to this question.

Explanation: The answer to this question is not one that is shown on the timeline. You will need to recall what you learned about the Erie Canal in fourth grade. The most important way that the Erie Canal opening helped New York's industries was that it became cheaper to transport goods. It was also much faster than other means of transportation. Another answer might be that we could now ship goods all the way from Buffalo to New York City easily.

Sample G

1. *Answer:* 1776

Explanation: The title of this picture gives the answer to this question.

2. *Answer:* Great Britain or England

Explanation: This question is more like a third question because you need to remember information from school. You need to remember that the Declaration of Independence was written and sent to England to declare that the colonists no longer wanted to be under their rule.

3. *Answer:* The Revolutionary War

Explanation: Again, this question asks for information that you learned in school. You will remember that the Declaration of Independence began the Revolutionary War, which was fought against England to gain independence for the colonies.

PRACTICE SET: DOCUMENT-BASED QUESTIONS AND ANSWERS

Beginning on the next page, you have a chance to try two complete DBQs from start to finish on your own. When you have finished, check the answers.

While you are working on these sample problems, it would be a great idea to pretend that you're taking the actual test. Sit down in a quiet place and time yourself as you complete this sample. You should give yourself 90 minutes to complete the whole DBQ, including the scaffolding questions and the essay.

Do not try to do both DBQs at the same time. Try sample DBQ 1 now, then read the answers and reflect on how you did. Adjust your strategies if you need to, and then on another day, try sample DBQ 2.

Good luck!

Sample DBQ 1

Directions: *The following essay task is based on Documents 1–5. You are to look at each document carefully and answer the question or questions that follow. Use your answers to the questions to help you write your essay on the following task.*

Historical background: The colonists of the 13 original colonies were subject to the rules and government of Great Britain. This was the case from the time of the first British colony until the Revolutionary Period.

Task:

For Part A, read each document carefully and answer the question or questions that follow. Then read the directions for Part B and write your essay.

For Part B, use the information from the documents, your answers to Part A, and your knowledge of social studies to write a well-organized essay. In your essay, you should:

Tell what events and ideas led the colonists to declare their independence from Great Britain and fight the Revolutionary War.

PART A: SHORT-ANSWER QUESTIONS

Directions: Read each document and answer the question or questions that follow. Answer the questions in the spaces provided.

Document 1

Selected Events Leading Up to the Revolutionary War

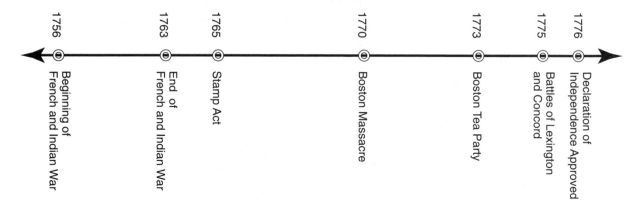

1. Was the Declaration of Independence approved before or after the Battles of Lexington and Concord?

Document 2

Declaration of Independence

We hold these truths to be self-evident, that all men are created equal, that they are endowed [given] by their Creator with certain unalienable Rights, that among these are Life, Liberty and the pursuit of Happiness. —That to secure these rights, Governments are instituted [made] among men, deriving [getting] their just powers from the consent [approval] of the governed. —That whenever any form of government becomes destructive of these ends, it is the right of the people to alter or to abolish it, and to institute [set up] a new government, laying its foundation on such principles [ideas] and organizing its powers in such form, as to them shall seem most likely to effect their safety and happiness.

Definitions:

Unalienable: cannot be taken away
Destructive: breaks or damages
Abolish: to get rid of

1. Name one right that the Declaration of Independence said that all men had.

   _____

2. According to the Declaration of Independence, when do the people have the right to set up a new government?

   _____
   _____
   _____
   _____

Document 3

Acts Passed by the British Parliament

Name of the Act	Year	Major Points
Sugar Act	1764	Taxed sugar, coffee, wine, other items.
The Stamp Act	1765	Taxed most printed materials including newspapers and legal documents.
The Quartering Act	1765	Stated that colonists must provide food, drink, fuel, places to sleep, and transportation to British soldiers.
The Townshend Acts	1767	Direct taxes on glass, lead, paper, paint, and tea. Lifted tax on tea for the British that imported it to the colonies. Stated that the New York Assembly must comply with the Quartering Act or they could not meet. Hired new people to oversee taxation, paid for by taxes.
The Intolerable Acts	1774	Closed Boston Harbor until the tea lost during the Boston Tea Party was paid for. Reduced Massachusetts to a crown colony; set up a military government. Allowed British official charged with a capital offense during law enforcement to go to England or another colony for a trial. Added new Quartering Act regulations.

1. Name three items that colonists were taxed on by the British.

_____

_____

_____

Document 4

During the Colonial period, many European countries claimed territories in the Americas including Spain, Great Britain, and France. The more colonial territory that a country had, the more powerful and potentially wealthy they were. It was this greed for control of territory that caused the French and Indian War. The war began because British settlers were settling farther and farther West, past the Ohio River valley and the Appalachian Mountains. France felt that this area of land belonged to them and wanted to push the British back East of the Appalachian Mountains. The war was fought from 1754 to 1759. The British had won. France gave Britain all territory East of the Mississippi River in North America; this included Canada. It was a large victory for the British, but one that had cost them many lives and large amounts of money. The British felt that since they were protecting the colonies, the colonists should help to pay back the large amounts of money that had been spent on the war. This was done through several new taxes on the colonists.

1. When the French and Indian War ended, what was one way that the British raised money to pay for the high costs of the war with France?

_____

_____

_____

Document 5

In March of 1770, a terrible event took place in Boston, Massachusetts. The event was called the Boston Massacre. A noisy group of colonists were teasing British soldiers. Things got out of control, and the fighting got worse in the panic. Five American colonists died, and seven were wounded. The patriots decided to make the most of this situation. Paul Revere made an engraving showing the Boston Massacre. It wasn't really accurate. It shows the Americans being peaceful and the British firing at them. The truth is that both sides were to blame. But Paul Revere's engraving was published throughout the colonies and helped to make people angry with the British.

1. Why did Paul Revere want to make the British soldiers look like they were firing at innocent people?

_____

_____

_____

_____

PART B: ESSAY

Directions: Write a well-organized essay using the documents, the answers to the questions in Part A, and your knowledge of social studies.

Historical background: The colonists of the 13 original colonies were subject to the rules and government of Great Britain. This was the case from the time of the first British colony until the Revolutionary Period.

Task:

Use the information from the documents in Part A and your knowledge of social studies to write a well-organized essay. In your essay, you should:

Tell what events and ideas led the colonists to declare their independence from Great Britain and fight the Revolutionary War.

Planning Page

Use this page to plan for your essay. Work on this page will not be counted toward your final score. Do not write your essay here.

Use the following space to write your essay.

Sample DBQ 1: Answers and Explanations

Document 1

1. *Answer:* The Declaration of Independence was approved after the Battles of Lexington and Concord.

Explanation: The Battles of Lexington and Concord are considered to be the first battles of the Revolutionary war. Because British were fighting against colonists, these events helped the colonies to decide to declare their independence from Great Britain.

Document 2

1. *Answer:* Any of the following choices would be acceptable: life, liberty, or the pursuit of happiness.

Explanation: This answer is found directly in the words of the Declaration of Independence.

2. *Answer:* People have the right to set up a new government when a government is not giving people their basic rights OR if a government is not getting its power from the support of the people.

Explanation: Either one of these answers is correct if you explained it clearly.

Document 3

1. *Answer/Explanation:* Any three of the following items is acceptable: sugar, coffee, wine, printed materials *or* newspapers, legal documents, glass, lead, paper, paint, or tea.

Document 4

1. *Answer/Explanation:* Taxes on the colonists

Document 5

1. *Answer/Explanation:* Paul Revere was a Patriot. He believed that the colonists were being treated unfairly by

Great Britain. The Boston Massacre engraving was a chance to make the British look bad by showing them firing at innocent colonists. Paul Revere hoped that this would convince more people to want to fight the British.

Sample Essay

In 1776 the American colonists approved the Declaration of Independence. This document explained that the colonists no longer wanted to be ruled by the British government. It explained that they wanted to set up their own government to give people the right to life, liberty, and the pursuit of happiness. This was a brave step that would change the colonies forever. Of course, the British did not give up without a fight, the Revolutionary War. Many people think that one event caused this war, but this is not true. Many events and ideas added up to cause it.

One of the most important issues related to the Revolutionary War was taxes. It all began because the British fought against the French and their Native American allies in the French and Indian War. This war was fought over land claims in the Americas. The British won this war, but it cost them a lot of money. The British government thought that the colonists should pay for the cost of the war and began to tax them heavily. One of those taxes was the Sugar Act of 1764. This placed taxes on sugar, coffee, wine, and other items. The colonists were not happy. Then in 1765, the Stamp Act was passed. It taxed most printed materials including newspaper and legal documents. These are just a few of the taxes that the colonists had to pay. The colonists thought that they did not have a say in how they were taxed and believed that this was unfair.

Another event that led to the Revolutionary War was the Boston Massacre. This took place in 1770. British soldiers killed five American colonists. Paul Revere made an engraving of it, and colonists all over saw it. This picture helped to make people even angrier with the British.

In addition to these events, there were some ideas that helped to convince the colonists that they should be free of British rule. These ideas are explained in the Declaration of Independence. The colonists believed that all men are created equal. They also believed that everyone had the right to life, to liberty, and to try to be happy. They explained that it is a government's job to make sure that this happens. If the government is not doing its job, then the people have the right to set up their own government. This is what they believed had happened in the colonies. They felt that the British government was not doing its job, so they wanted to set up their own government.

With all these events and ideas combined, it is easier to understand why the Revolutionary War happened. The colonists won the war, and the colonies became the United States of America.

Sample DBQ 2

Directions: The following essay task is based on Documents 1–5. This task is designed to test your ability to work with historical documents. Look at each document and answer the question or questions that follow. Use your answers to help you write your essay on the following task.

Historical background: Sometimes you hear people say that the world is shrinking. We know that they don't mean this literally. What they mean is that people from different places in the world are interdependent. They trade goods and services in a way that helps each of them. When you look around the room you are sitting in, you will probably see things made in many countries of the world. This is an example of interdependence.

Task:

For Part A, read each document carefully and answer the question or questions that follow. Then read the directions for Part B and write your essay.

For Part B, use the information from the documents, your answers to Part A, and your knowledge of social studies to write a well-organized essay. In your essay, you should:

Explain how people in the United States and other countries of the world are interdependent to meet their needs and wants.

PART A: SHORT-ANSWER QUESTIONS

Directions: Read each document and answer the question or questions that follow each document in the spaces provided.

Document 1

> Crude oil is a naturally occurring nonrenewable energy source. It is the raw material used to produce heating oils, gasoline, jet fuel, diesel fuel, asphalt, propane, and other products that are useful because they produce energy.

United States Crude Oil Imports—2006

Ranking	Country	Thousand Barrels
1	Canada	657,834
2	Mexico	575,501
3	Saudi Arabia	519,236
4	Venezuela	417,001
5	Nigeria	387,670
6	Iraq	201,866
7	Angola	187,325
8	Algeria	131,981
9	Ecuador	99,183
10	Kuwait	65,227
11	Colombia	51,630
12	Brazil	48,634
13	United Kingdom	47,271
14	Russia	39,253
15	Norway	35,897

Data Source: Energy Information Administration, U.S. Department of Energy

1. Name two countries that the United States imported crude oil from in 2006:

(a) _____

(b) _____

Document 2

Directions: *Please use your knowledge of social studies and the list below to answer Questions 1 and 2. Each item on the grocery list is followed by the name of the country from which it was imported.*

My Grocery List

Coffee - Costa Rica
Shrimp - Belize
Asparagus - Mexico
Apples - New York, USA
Beef Roast - Texas, USA
Gallon of Milk - New York, USA
Chocolate Bar - Switzerland
Cod - Iceland
Plums - Chile
Oranges - California, USA

1. Name two products on the grocery list that are produced in the United States:

   (a) _____

   (b) _____

2. Name two countries that produced items on the grocery list, other than the United States:

   (a) _____

   (b) _____

Document 3

Directions: *Please use your knowledge of social studies and the timeline below to answer Question 1.*

United States Free Trade Agreements (FTA)

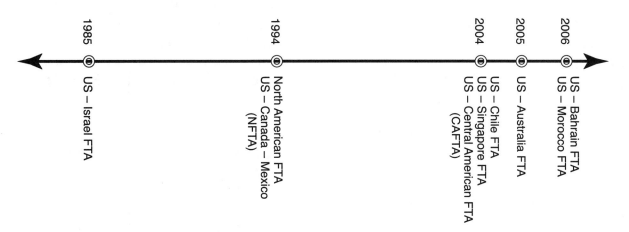

1985	US – Israel FTA
1994	North American FTA US – Canada – Mexico (NFTA)
2004	US – Chile FTA US – Singapore FTA US – Central American FTA (CAFTA)
2005	US – Australia FTA
2006	US – Bahrain FTA US – Morocco FTA

A free trade agreement (FTA) lowers or gets rid of completely the taxes that both countries have to pay to import or export goods to one another.

1. List two countries named on the timeline that the United States has free trade agreements with.

   (a) _____

   (b) _____

Document 4

Directions: *Please use your knowledge of social studies and the chart below to answer Questions 1 and 2.*

United States Imports and Exports of Selected Goods
Annual Report 2007
Reported in Millions of Dollars

Imports	Item	Exports
257	Corn	10,087
129,802	TV, VCRs	24,700
81,188	Clothing	3,199
97	Soy beans	10,014
245,777	Crude oil	993
28,055	Natural gas	3,019
13,298	Airplanes	51,894
31,807	Toys, games, and sporting goods	5,030
35,609	Scientific instruments	42,279

Data Source: Foreign Trade Division, U.S. Census Bureau
Data Not Seasonally Adjusted

1. Name one item that the United States imports more of than it exports.

_____

2. Name one item that the United States exports more of than it imports.

_____

Document 5

Directions: *Please use your knowledge of social studies and the press release below to answer Question 1.*

International Visitors Spent More in 2006 Than Ever Before

The U.S. Department of Commerce announced this week a record $107.4 billion in international travel receipts – which is travel-related tourism spending, including passenger fares – for the United States in 2006. This spending … surpasses the previous record of $103.1 billion set in 2000.

Purchases of travel and tourism-related goods and services by international visitors totaled $85.8 billion for the year, an increase of 5 percent over 2005. These goods and services include food, lodging, recreation, gifts, entertainment, local transportation in the United States, and other items incidental to international travel.

Passenger fares received by U.S. carriers and U.S. vessel operators from international visitors increased more than 3 percent over 2005 receipts to $21.6 billion for the year.

2006 U.S. Travel and Tourism Industry Highlights

- Travel and tourism supported 8.3 million American jobs in 2006, of which 1.1 million were supported by travel and tourism exports.
- More people are employed by travel and tourism-related industries than are employed in the construction industry, the business and financial industries, agriculture, education, or healthcare.

Office of Travel and Tourism Industries, 2/16/07

1. What is one benefit of tourism to the United States?

_____

_____

_____

PART B: ESSAY

Directions: In your own words, write a well-organized essay using the documents, the answers to the questions in Part A, and your knowledge of social studies.

Historical background: Sometimes you hear people say that the world is shrinking. We know that they don't mean this literally. What they mean is that people from different places in the world are interdependent. They trade goods and services, in a way that helps each of them. When you look around the room you are sitting in, you will probably see things made in many countries of the world. This is an example of interdependence.

Task:

Using information from the documents, and your knowledge of social studies, write an essay in which you:

Explain how people in the United States and other countries of the world are interdependent to meet their needs and wants.

In your essay, be sure to:

- Tell ways in which people in the United States and other countries of the world have become increasingly interdependent on each other to meet their needs and wants.
- Include an introduction, a body, and a conclusion.
- Use information from at least three documents in your answer.
- Include details, examples, or reasons in developing your ideas.

Planning Page

Use this page to plan for your essay. Work on this page will not be counted toward your final score. Do not write your essay here.

Use the following space to write your essay.

_____

_____

_____

_____

_____

_____

_____

_____

_____

_____

_____

_____

_____

_____

_____

_____

_____

_____

_____

_____

Sample DBQ 2: Answers and Explanations

Document 1

1. *Answer:* This question has several possible answers. You must have two countries from the following list: Canada, Mexico, Saudi Arabia, Venezuela, Nigeria, Iraq, Angola, Algeria, Ecuador, Kuwait, Colombia, Brazil, United Kingdom, Russia, or Norway.

Explanation: Be sure that you give two answers. The test will be scored so that each of the answers will earn credit, so by only listing one, you will lose points. The most logical answers would be Canada and Mexico as they are the top two countries that we import from and this may help you to explain your ideas in the essay later.

Document 2

1. *Answer:* You must have two items from the following list: coffee, shrimp, asparagus, chocolate bar, cod, or plums.

Explanation: These items are shown with a country of origin other than the United States. If you are confused about whether some of them are country names, you could use the process of elimination. All of those items produced in the United States are followed by USA; the above items are not.

2. *Answer:* You must have two countries from the following choices: Costa Rica, Belize, Mexico, Switzerland, Iceland, or Chile.

Explanation: These countries are shown as the country of origin for items on the grocery list. Be sure not to list the United States, as the question tells you not to. Also be sure that you list two countries.

Document 3

1. *Answer:* You must have two countries from the following list: Bahrain, Morocco, Australia, Chile, Singapore, Canada, Mexico, or Israel.

Explanation: Be sure that you list two countries. Also, you may know the countries of the CAFTA agreement, or there may be more free trade agreements not listed on the timeline; however, you cannot use those countries to answer this question because it specifically states that you must list countries named on the timeline.

Document 4

1. *Answer:* Any of the following choices are acceptable: TV, VCRs, clothing, crude oil, natural gas, or toys, games, and sporting goods.

Explanation: Look at the chart to determine the millions of dollars worth of imports and exports in the various categories. The question asks for items that the United States imports more of than it exports; this means that the value in the Imports column should be higher than the value in the Exports column. Be sure to refer to TV, VCRs as one item and toys, games, and sporting goods as one item. This is important because it is how they are listed on the chart.

2. *Answer:* Any of the following choices are acceptable: corn, soy beans, airplanes, or scientific instruments.

Explanation: The items listed above have higher dollar values in the Exports column than in the Imports column, making them the correct choice.

Document 5

1. *Answer:* There are many possible answers to this question. $107.4 billion was spent in the United States in 2006 due to tourism. Or, a record amount of money was spent in the United States in 2006 on tourism. Or, 8.3 million jobs are made possible in the United States by tourism. Or, more people are employed in travel and tourism-related industries than construction, business and financial industries, agriculture, education, or health care.

Explanation: All of the answer possibilities are not listed above, but your answer should explain something positive that happens because of tourism to the United States. It is a good idea to include a fact from the press release in your answer, as you are more likely to remember to use it in your essay if it is in your scaffolding answers.

Sample Essay

At some times in history, people were completely self-sufficient. They grew their own food, built their own homes, and found ways to meet their own needs and wants. This isn't the case anymore. The countries of the world are interdependent on each other. That means that we provide people with some of the things they need or want and we get other things that we need or want from other countries. In our world today, there are many examples of this interdependence.

One example of a way in which the United States relies on other countries of the world is for some types of energy that we use. For example, we import very large amounts of crude oil. Crude oil is the raw material used to make gasoline, heating oils, propane, and more. In 2006, we purchased the largest amount of crude oil from our two closest neighbors, Canada and Mexico. We imported 657,834 thousand barrels of crude oil from Canada alone. Looking more recently at 2007, you can see that we exported 993 million dollars worth of crude oil, yet purchased 245,777 million dollars worth of crude oil. This shows that we need other countries for our gasoline- and crude oil-based fuels. Another example of an energy source that we import more of than we export is natural gas. In 2007, we exported 3,019 million dollars worth of natural gas and imported much more, 28,055 million dollars worth. As you can see, we need other countries in the world for many of our energy needs.

The world is interdependent, which means that we trade with each other to get the things that we need and want. Countries of the world export the things that they have a lot of or can produce, and import those things that they cannot produce, or need more of than they have. There are things that the United States exports to other countries and things that we import. Some things that we imported more of than we exported in 2007 were TVs, VCRs, clothing, toys, games, and sporting goods. These items were made in other countries, such as China, and brought to our country to be sold. We don't import everything though. There are some things that we produce and export to other countries to sell to them. Some examples of this are scientific instruments, airplanes, and many foods. We trade to get what we want, but because of fast and cheap transportation, we can trade with people all over the world.

Have you taken a look at your local grocery store lately? Food is an excellent example of a way the world is interdependent. At your grocery store, you might find shrimp from Belize, chocolate from Switzerland, and plums from Chile. These foods will be sitting right there next to an apple grown at an orchard in your town or milk from a local dairy. What is fascinating is that some of the food we grow locally is exported and sold to other countries around the world to be sold in their grocery stores. For example, in 2007 the United States exported over 10,000 million dollars worth of corn, something we can grow in our own yards in New York State. We also export soy beans and other foods. Being able to trade food gives us many more choices at our grocery store.

In order to buy the things that we need and want, we need to have a way to make money. Tourism is another way that the world is interdependent. In 2006, travel to the United States, the places those visitors stayed, food they ate, and things they bought totaled $85.8 billion for the year! That money is used to pay people who work in tourism-related jobs and there are over 8 million of those. Because of easier and cheaper travel, people are able to visit here and spend money, which is good for us. When Americans earn money and have jobs, they may use some of that money to visit other countries in the world and buy goods from those countries. It helps everyone.

When you think about the world today, we are very connected and interdependent. It is like a web of trade and travel. One reason might be some of the agreements that the United States has made with other countries about trade. For example, we have free trade agreements with countries like Australia, Chile, Israel, and many more. These free trade agreements make it easier for the countries to sell goods to each other, by having low or no taxes on imports. But whatever the reason, it is very clear that countries of the world are not self-sufficient anymore. Trade allows us to get things that we need or want from other places and then sell other countries the things we have or make. We rely on each other, that is what we mean when we say the world is interdependent.

This essay would earn a score of 4 out of 4. It is well organized, detailed, and clear. The writing is in the author's own words and not copied directly from the documents or questions. This is important because it shows that you really understand the documents and questions. The essay uses information from all of the documents; important because the directions tell you to use information from at least three. This essay clearly answers the question asked.

Index